AF380534

THE PARABLES OF JESUS
SERMONS BY SAINT GREGORY PALAMAS

THE PARABLES OF JESUS
Sermons by Saint Gregory Palamas

edited by
Christopher Veniamin

MOUNT THABOR PUBLISHING
2022

THE PARABLES OF JESUS: SERMONS BY SAINT GREGORY PALAMAS
Copyright © 2022 by Christopher Veniamin

First edition 2013
First Reprint edition (with minor corrections) 2022

Mount Thabor Publishing
106 Hilltop Road
Dalton, PA 18414 USA

www.mountthabor.com

Printed in the United States of America

All rights reserved. No part of this publication may be reproduced,
stored in a retrieval system, or transmitted, in any form or by any means,
electronic, mechanical, photocopying, recording, or otherwise, without
the prior permission of Mount Thabor Publishing.

Library of Congress Cataloging-in-Publication Data

Gregory Palamas, Saint, 1296-1359.
[Homilies. English. Selections. 2013]
The parables of Jesus : sermons by Saint Gregory Palamas / edited by
Christopher Veniamin. -- 1st ed.
     p. cm.
ISBN 978-0-9774983-7-6 (alk. paper)
1. Jesus Christ--Parables--Sermons. 2. Orthodox Eastern Church--
Sermons--Early works to 1800. 3. Sermons, Greek--Translations into
English. I. Veniamin, Christopher, 1958- II. Title.
BT375.3.G74313 2011
226.8'06--dc22

                    2010013532

Front cover:
Tax collector and Pharisee. Byzantine fresco, 1410-1418.
Photo Credit : Erich Lessing / Art Resource, NY
Monastery, Manasija, Serbia

Σωφρονίῳ Ἀθωνίτῃ
(1896 – 1993)

Saint Gregory Palamas
(1296–1359)
Chapel of the Holy Unmercenary Physicians
Vatopedi Monastery, Mount Athos

Luminary of the Orthodox faith,
support of the Church and teacher,
splendour of monastics,
invincible champion of theologians,
O wonderworker Gregory,
boast of Thessalonica,
preacher of grace,
pray without ceasing
that our souls be saved.

Dismissal Hymn (*Apolytikion*) of the Saint
Fourth Plagial (Tone Eight), Second Sunday in Great Lent

Contents

Foreword

THE PARABLES OF JESUS is the fourth volume in the series *Sermons by Saint Gregory Palamas,* the purpose of which is to bring the life and teaching of this remarkable fourteenth century saint (1296–1359) to a wider readership, to the layperson interested in the rich Biblical tradition of the Church Fathers.

Arranged thematically, the work in hand consists of seven sermons on the Lord's parables. Placed in liturgical sequence and according to their corresponding numbers in the corpus, these homilies include the parable of the Publican and the Pharisee (Homily 2), of the Prodigal Son (Homily 3), of the Second Coming (Homily 4), of the Unforgiving Servant (Homily 36), of the Marriage Feast (Homily 41), of the Sower (Homily 47), and of Lazarus and the Rich Man (Homily 48) .

It was in 1334, while on Mount Athos, in his third year at the hermitage of Saint Sabas, which belongs to the Great Lavra, that Palamas experienced a vision in which he was encouraged to share the wisdom bestowed upon him from on high. It seemed that he was carrying a vessel overflowing with milk, which subsequently turned into the finest of wines. The wine emitted such a strong fragrance that it brought great joy to his soul. A youth appeared and rebuked him for not sharing the wine with others and for allowing it to go to waste, for this wine, as he explained, was inexhaustible. The angel then warned Gregory, reminding him of the parable of the talents (*cf.* Matt. 25:14–30). As he later related to his friend and disciple Dorotheus,[1] Palamas understood this vision to mean that the time would come when he would be called upon to transfer his teaching from the simple plane of the ethical (the milk) to the higher plane of the dogmatic word (the wine), which leads heavenward.[2] Thus at the age of about thirty-eight Gregory began to write his Encomium for Saint Peter the Athonite, and, at about the same time, he also began to compose what is without doubt the most famous of all his works, Homily 53, "On the Entry of the Mother of God into the Holy of Holies", in which the *Theotokos* is presented as the archetype of the hesychastic way of life, the way of "stillness" (Gk. *hesychia*, *cf.* Ps. 46:10).

The teaching of Saint Gregory and his fellow Hesychasts was based on the understanding that man, the greatest of all God's creatures, had been called to enter into direct and unmediated communion with God even from this present life. The chief manner by which this is achieved is through the grace of God and *noetic* prayer, that is, through the Prayer of the Heart, also known as the Jesus Prayer: *Lord Jesus Christ, Son of God, have mercy upon me.* For the Hesychasts, therefore, true theology, real knowledge of God, is given not to those whose minds have been exercised in lofty concepts *about* God, but to those who, through prayer and ascetic striving in accordance with the commandments of Christ, have been made worthy to behold the vision of Christ in glory, to those who have seen God face to face and share in His very Life.

---

1. One of the Vlatte brothers (the other being Markos), who built Vlattadon Monastery (1351–1371). Dorotheus later also served as Archbishop of Thessalonica, from 1371 to 1379.

2. Philotheus Kokkinos, *Encomium for our father among the saints, Gregory Palamas, Archbishop of Thessalonica,* ed. J.-P. Migne, *Patrologia Graeca* 151:580A–581B; see esp. crit. ed. Demetrios G. Tsames, *The Hagiological Works of Philotheus Kokkinos, Patriarch of Constantinople,* vol. 1: *Thessalonian Saints,* Center for Byzantine Studies (Thessalonica, 1985), §§ 36–37, pp. 467–468.

Text and Translation

The present work is based on the edition of Panagiotes K. Chrestou.[3] The initial translation of the sermons contained in *On the Saints* was kindly made available to the editor for correction and improvement by Archimandrite Zacharias of the Holy Monastery of St. John the Baptist, England, and subsequently corrected against the original Greek, oftentimes reworked, and given its present form. Responsibility for the final version of the text, of course, rests entirely with the editor.

I wish to express my deepest gratitude to Abbot Ephraim and the brethren of the Holy Monastery of Vatopedi on Mount Athos for so kindly providing me with a copy of the oldest extant icon of St. Gregory: a 1371 wall-painting from the Chapel of the Holy Unmercenary Physicians (Gk. *Anargyroi*) at Vatopedi (see back cover and p. vi). The front cover icon is a 1410–1418 Byzantine fresco from Manasija Monastery in Serbia.

A Note on Biblical References

Even though Saint Gregory himself used the Septuagint (Greek) text of the Old Testament, for purely practical reasons I have considered it expedient to employ the numbering, names, and wording of the Hebrew (Massoretic) text, as found in the more familiar Authorized (King James) Version. Scriptural quotations have been adjusted in favour of the Septuagint rendering only where significant differences occur. Such instances have been indicated by the use of Lxx.

C. V.

SAINT TIKHON'S ORTHODOX THEOLOGICAL SEMINARY
PASCHA, FEAST *of* FEASTS, 2010

---

3. *Gregory Palamas: The Complete Works*, vols. 9–11, in the series *Greek Fathers of the Church*, nos. 72, 76, and 79 (Thessalonica, 1985–1986), with an accompanying Modern Greek rendering. This was in fact the preliminary text of Professor Vasileios S. Pseutonkas' critical edition (2015), which is now the sixth and final volume in Chrestou's Γρηγορίου τοῦ Παλαμᾶ· Συγγράμματα [Gregory Palamas: The Writings] (Thessalonica, 1962ff).

On the Lord's Parable
Of the Publican and the Pharisee

THE UNSEEN PATRON OF EVIL is full of evil ingenuity. Right at the beginning he can drag away, by means of hopelessness and lack of faith, the foundations of virtue already laid in the soul. Again, by means of indifference and laziness, he can make an attempt on the walls of virtue's house just when they are being built up. Or he can bring down the roof of good works after its construction, by means of pride and madness. But stand firm, do not be alarmed, for a diligent man is even more ingenious in good things, and virtue has superior forces to deploy against evil. It has at its disposal supplies and support in battle from Him who is all-powerful, who in His goodness strengthens all lovers of virtue. So not only can virtue remain unshaken by the various wicked devices prepared by the enemy, but it can also lift up and restore those fallen into the depths of evil, and easily lead them to God by repentance and humility.

Here is an example and a clear proof. The publican, as a publican, dwells in the depths of sin. All he has in common with those who live virtuously is one short utterance, but he finds relief, is lifted up and rises above every evil. He is numbered with the company of the righteous, justified by the impartial Judge Himself. If the Pharisee is condemned by his speech, it is because, as a Pharisee, he thinks himself somebody, although he is not really righteous, and utters many arrogant words which provoke God's anger with their every syllable.

Why does humility lead up to the heights of righteousness, whereas self-conceit leads down to the depths of sin? Because anybody who thinks he is something great, even before God, is rightly abandoned by God, as one who thinks that he does not need His help. Anybody who despises himself, on the other hand, and relies on mercy from above, wins God's sympathy, help and grace. As it says, "The Lord resisteth the proud: but he giveth grace unto the lowly" (Prov. 3:34 Lxx).

The Lord demonstrates this in a parable, saying, "Two men went up into the temple to pray, the one a Pharisee, and the other a publican" (Luke 18:10). Wanting to set clearly before us the gain that comes from humility and the loss from pride, he divided into two groups all who went to the Temple, or, rather, those who went up into the Temple, who are the ones who go there to pray. This is the nature of prayer, it brings a man up from the earth into heaven and, rising above every heavenly name, height and honour, sets him before the God who is over all (*cf.* Rom. 9:5). The ancient Temple was set in a high place, on a hill above the city. Once when a deadly epidemic was destroying Jerusalem, David saw the Angel of Death on this hill, stretching out his sword against the city. He went up there and built an altar to the Lord, on which he offered a sacrifice to God, and the destruction ceased (2 Sam. 24:15–25). All these things are an image of the saving ascent of the spirit during holy prayer and of the forgiveness it brings – for these things all foreshadowed our salvation. They can also be an image of this holy church of ours, which is indeed set in a high place, in another angelic country above the world, where the great, bloodless sacrifice, acceptable to God, is offered for the forgiveness of the whole world, the destruction of death and abundance of eternal life.

So the Lord did not say, "Two men went to the temple", but "went up" into the Temple. Even now there are some who come to the holy church without going up. Instead they bring down the church, the image of heaven. They come for the sake of meeting each other and talking, or to buy and sell goods, and they resemble each other, for the latter offer goods, the former words, and all receive a fair exchange.

As in those days the Lord drove them completely out of the Temple saying, "My house shall be called the house of prayer; but ye have made it a den of thieves" (Matt. 21:13), so He also drove them away from their conversations as they did not really go up into the Temple at all, even if they came there every day.

The Pharisee and the publican went up into the Temple, both with the aim of praying. But the Pharisee brought himself down after going up, defeating his aim by the way he prayed. Both had the same aim in going up, both went up to pray, but they prayed in opposite ways. One made the ascent broken and contrite, for he had learned from the psalmist and prophet that "a broken and a contrite heart, O God, thou wilt not despise" (Ps. 51:17). The prophet says of himself, with the knowledge of experience, "I was brought low and the Lord helped me" (Ps. 116:6). But why am I talking about the prophet, when the God of the prophets, who for our sake became like us, humbled himself. "Wherefore", as the apostle says, "God hath highly exalted him" (Phil. 2:9). The Pharisee, by contrast, goes up bloated with pretensions to justify himself in the presence of God, although all our righteousness is like a filthy rag before Him (cf. Isa. 64:6). He had not heard the saying, "Everyone that is proud in heart is an abomination to the Lord" (Prov. 16:5), or, "God resisteth the proud" (Prov. 3:34 Lxx), or, "Woe unto them that are wise in their own eyes, and prudent in their own sight" (Isa. 5:21).

The two were different not only in their manner and way of praying but also in their type of prayer, for there are two kinds. Prayer is not only a matter of entreaty but also of thanksgiving. Of those who pray, one goes up to the Temple of God praising and thanking God for what he has received from him. Another asks for what he has not yet received, including, in the case of those of us who sin all the time, remission of sins. When we piously promise to offer something to God, that is not called prayer but a vow, as shown by the one who said, "Vow, and pay unto the Lord your God" (Ps. 76:11), and the other who said, "Better is it that thou shouldest not vow, than that thou shouldest vow and not pay" (Eccles. 5:4).

However, these two kinds of prayer can both be unprofitable for the unwary. Faith and contrition make prayer and supplication for the remission of sins effective, once evil deeds have been renounced, but despair and hardness of heart make it ineffectual. Thanksgiving for the benefits received from God is made acceptable by humility and not looking down on those who lack them. It is rendered unacceptable, however, by being conceited, as if those benefits resulted from our own efforts and knowledge, and by condemning those who have not received them. The Pharisee's behaviour and words prove he was afflicted with both these diseases. He went up to the Temple to give thanks, not to make supplication and, like a wretched fool, mingled conceit and condemnation of others with his thanksgiving. For he stood and prayed thus with himself: "God, I thank thee, that I am not as other men are, extortioners, unjust, adulterers" (Luke 18:11).

Instead of the attitude of a servant, the Pharisee's stance displays shameless self-exaltation, the opposite of that other man who, in his humility, did not dare to lift up his eyes to heaven. It stands to reason that the Pharisee prayed to himself, for his prayer did not ascend to God, although it did not escape the notice of Him who sits upon the cherubim and observes the lowest depths of the abyss. When he said "I thank thee", he did not go on to say, "because in Thy mercy Thou didst freely deliver me, weak and unable to fight as I am, from the snares of the devil". For he is spiritually courageous who manages to take refuge in repentance when caught in the snares of the enemy and fallen into the nets of sin. The circumstances of our lives are directed by a higher providence and often, with little or no effort on our part, by God's help we have stayed out of reach of many great passions, delivered by His sympathy for our weakness. We should acknowledge the gift and humble ourselves before the giver, not be conceited.

The Pharisee says, "I thank thee, God", not because I have received any help from Thee, but "because I am not as other men are". As though it was from his own resources and through his own ability that he was not an extortioner or unjust or an adulterer – if, indeed, he really was not. He did not pay attention to himself, or he would not have said he was righteous. He was looking more at everyone else than at himself and, in his madness, despised them all. Only one seemed to him to be righteous and chaste: himself. "I am not", he says, "as other men are, extortioners, unjust, adulterers, or even as this publican" (Luke 18:11). Anyone could point out to him how foolish he was, by saying to him, "If all except yourself are unjust and extortioners, then who are the victims of extortion and injustice? What about this publican, and the extra words you added about him? Since he is one of the rest, surely he was included in your general, your universal, condemnation? Or did he have to be condemned twice over because he was in your sight, even though he was standing far away from you. You knew he was unjust because he was obviously a publican, but how did you know he was an adulterer? Or perhaps you are entitled to treat him unjustly and insult him since he treated others unjustly?" But it is not so. With a humble mind he bears your arrogant accusation and, reproaching himself, he offers supplication to God and is delivered by Him from the condemnation of having treated others unjustly. You, however, will be rightly condemned for having arrogantly made accusations against him and all men, and deemed only yourself righteous. "I am not as other men are, extortioners, unjust, adulterers."

These words show the Pharisee's disdain for God and for everybody, but also for the standards of his own conscience. He openly despises everybody and ascribes his abstention from evil not to God's strength but to his own. If he says that he thanks God, it is only because he considers all men apart from himself to be licentious, unjust and extortioners, as though God saw fit to grant virtue to him alone. However, if everyone were like that, all the Pharisee's goods would be in their possession as loot. But this is not so, for he adds, "I fast twice in the week, I give tithes of all that I gain" (Luke 18:12). He does not say that he gives tithes of all that he possesses, but of all that he gains, meaning the additions and increases to his fortune. So he kept what he possessed and also took without hindrance as much as he could over and above that. How could all except himself be extortioners and unjust? This is how self-confuting and self-deceiving evil is! Madness is always mixed with lies.

He put forward the fact that he gave tithes of his wealth to prove his righteousness; for if someone gives tithes of his own wealth how can he be an extortioner of other people's? He put forward fasting to show off his chastity because fasting gives rise to purity. For argument's sake, then, let us say you are chaste, righteous, wise, sensible, brave, and whatever else you wish. If this has come from yourself and not from God, why do you deceitfully pretend to pray? Why do you go up into the Temple and give thanks in vain? But if it has come from God, you did not receive it so as to boast but for the edification of others to the glory of the giver. You should have humbly rejoiced and given thanks both to Him who gave and to those for whose sake the gifts were given. The lamp receives light for those who see it, not for itself. For "week" the Pharisee uses the word "sabbath", but he means not the seventh day but the seven days, on two of which he brags that he fasts. He is unaware that such fasts are mere human virtues, whereas pride is demonic. When pride is linked with fasting, however genuine, it annuls and destroys the virtues, and how much more so if the fasting is a sham.

These are the words of the Pharisee. By contrast, the publican "standing afar off, would not lift up so much as his eyes unto heaven, but smote upon his breast saying, God be merciful to me a sinner" (Luke 18:13). See the extent of his humility, faith and self-reproach. See the utter abasement of his thoughts and feelings, and, at the same time, contrition of heart mingled with this publican's prayer. When he went up into the Temple to pray for the remission of his sins, he brought with him good advocates before God: unashamed faith, uncondemned self-reproach, contrition of heart that is not despised and humility that exalts. He linked attention to prayer most excellently. It says, "The publican standing afar off". Not "stood", as in the case of the Pharisee, but "standing", to show that he was standing for a long time continuously praying and asking for mercy. Without any other intention or thought he paid attention only to himself and God, turning over and repeating the supplication of a single thought, the most effective of all prayers.

"And the publican, standing afar off, would not lift up so much as his eyes unto heaven" (Luke 18:13). As he stood he bowed down, and his bearing was not only that of a lowly servant, but also of a condemned man. It also proclaims a soul delivered from sin. Although still far from God, without the boldness towards Him that comes from good works, it hopes to draw near to him because it has already renounced evil and is intent on good. "Standing afar off the publican would not lift up so much as his eyes unto heaven", showing his self-condemnation and self-reproach by his manner and appearance. He saw himself as unworthy either of heaven or of the earthly Temple, so he stood on the threshold of the Temple, not daring even to turn his gaze towards heaven, still less towards the God of heaven. In his intense contrition he smote upon his breast to show he was worthy of punishment. He sighed in deepest mourning, bowing his head like a condemned man, calling himself a sinner and begging with faith for forgiveness, saying, "God be merciful to me a sinner". For he believed Him who said, "Turn ye unto me, and I will turn unto you" (Zech. 1:3), and the prophet who bore witness, "I said, I will confess my transgressions unto the Lord, and thou forgavest the iniquity of my heart" (*cf.* Ps. 32:5).

What happened then? "This man", says the Lord, "went down to his house justified rather than the other, for every one that exalteth himself shall be abased; and he that humbleth himself shall be exalted" (Luke 18:14). As the devil is conceit itself and pride is his own particular evil, it defeats and swallows up any human virtue with which it is mixed. Whereas humility is the virtue of the good angels, and defeats any human evil that comes upon fallen mankind. Humility is the chariot by which we ascend to God, like those clouds which are to carry up to God those who would dwell for endless ages with Him, as foretold by the apostle: "We shall be caught up in the clouds to meet the Lord in the air: and so shall we ever be with the Lord" (1 Thess. 4:17). Humility is the same as such a cloud. It is formed by repentance, releases streams of tears; brings out the worthy from among the unworthy and leads them up to unite them with God, justified by His free gift for the gratitude of their free disposition.

At first the publican evilly appropriated other people's goods; later he renounced dishonesty and by not justifying himself, was justified. The Pharisee did not lay claim to other people's possessions, but by justifying himself he was condemned. What will befall those who do lay claim to other people's possessions and attempt to justify themselves?

Let us leave them, as the Lord does, for words will not convince such people. Sometimes it happens that we humble ourselves when we pray, and we may imagine that we shall be rewarded with the same justification as the publican. But it is not so. We must consider the fact that the publican was despised by the Pharisee to his face, even after he had abandoned sin, and he condemned himself with contempt, not only not contradicting the Pharisee but joining in with his accusations against him.

When you abandon your evildoing, do not contradict those who despise or reproach you because of it. Join them in condemning yourself for what you are like and, through contrite prayer, take refuge in the forgiveness of God alone, realizing that you are a rescued publican. Many have called themselves sinners, and so do we, but dishonour tests the heart. The great Paul is far removed from pharisaic boasting, but he wrote to those in Corinth who were speaking in tongues, "I thank my God, I speak with tongues more than ye all" (1 Cor. 14:18). (He who elsewhere calls himself the offscouring of all things, writes these words to restrain those who look down on those who did not have this gift, *cf.* 1 Cor. 4:13). If therefore Paul, who is far removed from pharisaic boasting, can write such words, it is also possible for someone to say the same words as the publican and be humble in speech like him, but not to be justified as he was. To the publican's words must be added his renunciation of evil, his soul's disposition, his contrition and his patience. David shows us by his actions that anyone who considers himself guilty before God and repents must believe that the reproach and contempt of others towards him is just and to be endured. After he had sinned, when he heard Shimei speaking ill of him, he said to those who wanted to retaliate, "Let him curse, because the Lord hath said unto him, Curse David" (2 Sam. 16:10). According to him, God's forgiveness of David's sin against him had posted the man there. Yet David was struggling at that time with a great and terrible calamity, as Absalom had just risen up in revolt against him (2 Sam. 15:7ff).

Leaving Jerusalem against his will and with unbearable grief, he fled as far as the foot of the Mount of Olives. There, to make the calamity worse, he met Shimei throwing stones at him, cursing him mercilessly and insulting him shamelessly (2 Sam. 16:5ff). He called him a bloodthirsty man and a criminal, as if to remind the king, to his disgrace, of the incident with Bathsheba and Uriah (2 Sam. 11:3–15). He did not stop after cursing him once or twice and throwing a few stones, and words that strike harder than stones. It says the king with all his men went on with Shimei going along the mountainside following the king, cursing him, throwing stones from the side and spattering him with mud. The king did not lack men to stop him. Abishai, his commander, unable to endure it, said to the king, "Why should this dead dog curse my lord and king? let me go over, I pray thee, and take off his head" (2 Sam. 16:9). But David restrained him and all his servants, saying to them, "Let him curse. It may be that the Lord will look on my affliction, and that the Lord will requite me good for his cursing this day" (2 Sam. 16:12).

The happenings which took place in those days are shown in the parable of the publican and the Pharisee, fulfilled for ever by righteousness. If someone really accounts himself guilty of eternal punishment, he will courageously endure not just dishonour but also harm, disease and, in fact, every kind of misfortune and ill-treatment. He who shows such patience, as though in debt and guilty, is delivered by a very light condemnation, temporary and ephemeral, from truly grievous, unbearable and unending punishment. Sometimes he may even be delivered from dangers threatening him now, because God's kindness begins from that point, due to his patience. Someone chastened by God said, "I will bear the chastening of the Lord, because I have sinned against him" (cf. Micah 7:9 Lxx).

May we, chastened not by the Lord's wrath and anger but by His mercy, not be cast down by God's punishment, but like the psalmist may we be raised up at the end by the grace and love towards mankind of our Lord Jesus Christ, to whom be glory, might, honour and worship, together with the Father and the life-giving Spirit, now and for ever and unto the ages of ages. Amen.

On the Parable
Of the Prodigal who was Saved

"Behold the days come, that there will be famine", says the prophet as he weeps for Jerusalem, "not a famine of bread, nor a thirst for water, but of hearing the word of the Lord" (Amos 8:11). Famine means being deprived of and desiring necessary food. But there is something worse and more wretched than this famine: when someone is deprived of the necessary means of salvation and does not perceive his misfortune, having no desire to be saved. Someone who is hungry and in need goes round searching everywhere for a crust of bread. If he finds some mouldy barley bread, or someone offers him bread made from millet or husks, or any other lowly kind of food, his joy equals his former anguish when he could not find anything. The person suffering from spiritual famine, being deprived of and desiring spiritual nourishment, goes round searching for someone with God's gift of teaching. If he finds someone, he joyfully feeds on the bread of spiritual life, the word of salvation, which nobody who keeps searching to the end fails to find. As Christ says, "Every one that asketh receiveth; and he that seeketh findeth; and to him that knocketh it shall be opened" (Luke 11:10).

Some people, because their minds have gone so long without nourishment, lose their desire to eat and so do not notice the harm they are suffering. If they have a teacher it annoys them to listen to him. If they do not, they do not look for someone to instruct them, and live more sinfully than the prodigal. Although by going away he deprived himself of the Provider, Father and Lord of us all, when he was caught in a terrible famine and perceived his deprivation, he repented, went back, searched and found again the divine and undefiled nourishment. Through repentance he benefited so greatly from the gifts of the Spirit that he was envied for his riches.

But let us go back to the beginning and expound to you in your charity this parable of the Lord in the Gospel, as it is customary to read it in church today.

"A certain man", it says, "had two sons" (Luke 15:11). Here in the parable the Lord calls Himself a man. There is nothing strange in this. If He truly became man for our salvation, it is not at all strange if He presents Himself as one particular man for our benefit. He is the eternal Guardian of our souls and bodies, of which He is Creator and Lord, and He has shown surpassing love and care towards us in His works, even before we came into being.

Before we existed, from the foundation of the world, He prepared a kingdom for us to inherit, as He tells us Himself (Matt. 25:34). Before we existed for our sake he made the angels ministering spirits, as Paul says, "sent forth to minister for them who shall be heirs of salvation" (Heb. 1:14). Before we existed for our sake he stretched out the heavens over the whole visible world, as if putting up a tent for us without distinction in this transitory life. The heavens themselves are perpetually in motion, full of movement and unmoving. Unmoving in that they do not suddenly change and bring destruction on the inhabitants of the earth. Full of movement because they are held in place by counterbalancing movements. Perpetually in motion as they carry with them the multitude of stars in set order, that we might learn how transitory our life is, and also enjoy all the heavenly bodies in turn as they pass above our heads. Before we existed for our sake He made the greater light to rule the day and the lesser light to rule the night (Gen. 1:16). He set them and the stars in the firmament of heaven to move in the same and in the opposite direction, existing together and differing from one another in their various kinds, that they might be for signs both for seasons and for years. None of these signs are necessary to the spiritual creation, which is above the senses, or to the animals, which live by their senses alone. They were made for us, who by our senses enjoy the other benefits of the visible world as well as its beauty, while in our minds we can apprehend the signs we see.

For our sake before we existed He laid the foundations of the earth, spread out the sea upon them, poured out air in abundance over everything and above the air kindled fire in His wisdom, that the excessive cold of what lay below might be tempered by having fire all around, while the fire's own excessive heat would be contained in one place. If all this was also necessary for the animals to survive, yet they too were made, before we existed, for the service of man, as the prophet David sings in the Psalms (Ps. 104:14).

To sustain our bodies our Creator brought this whole world out of nothing before He created us. But to improve our ways and lead us towards virtue there is nothing our benevolent Lord did not do. He made all the visible world like a mirror of heavenly things, so that by contemplating it spiritually we might attain to them as by a marvellous ladder. He put in each of us a natural law, our own conscience, as a steady plumbline, an upright judge and an unerring teacher. If we concentrate our minds within ourselves, we will need no other teacher to understand what is good. If, through our senses, we rightly turn our mind outside ourselves, "the invisible things of God are clearly seen, being understood by the things that are made", as the apostle says (Rom. 1:20).

When, by means of nature and creation, He had opened the school of virtues, he appointed guardian angels over us, raised up fathers and prophets as our guides and showed signs and wonders to lead us to faith. He gave us the written law to assist the law implanted in our reasonable nature and the teaching given by creation. In the end, as we treated everything with scorn – how great is our laziness, and what a contrast with the long-suffering and care of Him who loves us! – He gave Himself to us for our sake. Emptying the riches of the Godhead into our lowest depths, he took our nature and, becoming a man like us, was called our teacher. He Himself teaches us about His great love for mankind, demonstrating it by word and deed, while at the same time leading his followers to imitate His compassion and turn away from hardness of heart.

Tender love is found in people who have things in their care, so shepherds love their sheep and owners love their property. Since, however, such love is greater between those linked by blood and kinship, and greatest of all between fathers and their own children, the Lord uses these latter to demonstrate His own love for mankind, calling Himself a man and the father of us all. For He was made a man for our sake and gave us new birth through holy baptism and the accompanying grace of the Holy Spirit.

"A certain man", it says, "had two sons". For the difference in minds divided a single nature into two, and the distinction between good and evil gathered many people into two. We sometimes say something is twofold when it has two different modes of conduct, even though it is essentially one, or again, we call many people a single entity, when they are all of one accord. "And the younger of them said to his father" (Luke 15:12). It stands to reason that he was the younger, for he makes a childish and very foolish request. The sin which he had in his mind as he hatched his plan to depart is itself younger than virtue, being a later invention of our evil inclinations. Virtue, by contrast, is ancient, for it was eternally with God, and was instilled in our soul from the beginning by the grace of God.

"The younger of them", it says, "came and said to his father, give me the portion of goods that falleth to me." What foolishness! He did not fall down at his father's feet beseeching him, he simply said it. Moreover, he demands his portion like a debt from Him who graciously gives to everyone. "Give me the portion of goods which legally belongs to me, my just share." By which law and which justice are fathers in debt to their children? Quite the opposite: children are in debt to their fathers, as nature proves, for they owe their existence to them. This too shows his childish frame of mind.

What does He do who sends rain on the just and the unjust, who makes the sun rise on the evil and the good (Matt. 5:45)? "He divided unto them his living" (Luke 15:12). Note that this man, the father, needs nothing for himself. Otherwise he would not have divided his living just between the two of them, or just into two portions, but would have kept back a third portion for himself. Being God, "He has no need of our good things", as David says (Ps. 15:2 Lxx). So he divided his living, which means the whole world, between these two sons. As the one nature is divided by two differing minds, so the one world is put to two differing uses. One person says to God, "All the day long I have stretched forth my hands unto thee" (Ps. 88:9), "Seven times a day do I praise thee" (Ps. 119:164), "At midnight I will rise to give thanks unto thee" (Ps. 119:62), "At the last hour I cried unto the Lord" (Ps. 119:1 Lxx), "I trust in thy words" (Ps. 119:42) and "I will early destroy all the wicked of the land" (Ps. 101:8), meaning he will cut off the longings of the flesh that lead to sensual pleasure. Another spends all day over his wine and looking for places to drink. His nights are passed in impure and lawless actions and he rushes headlong into concealed dangers, or obvious treacheries, robberies and evil projects. Yet both shared the same night, the same sun and, most importantly, the same nature, exploiting it in opposite ways. God has divided the whole creation equally to all, offering it to each to use as he pleases.

"And not many days after", it says, "the younger son gathered all together, and took his journey into a far country" (Luke 15:13). Why did he not set off at once instead of a few days after? The evil prompter, the devil, does not simultaneously suggest to us that we should do what we like and that we should sin. Instead he cunningly beguiles us little by little, whispering, "Even if you live independently without going to God's Church or listening to the Church teacher, you will still be able to see for yourself what your duty is and not depart from what is good." When he separates someone from the divine services and obedience to the holy teachers, he also distances him from God's vigilance and surrenders him to evil deeds. God is everywhere present. Only one thing is far away from His goodness: evil. Being in the power of evil through sin we set off on a journey far away from God. As David says to God, "The evil shall not stand in thy sight" (Ps. 5:5).

Once the younger son had gone away and taken his journey into a far country, "there he dispersed his substance with riotous living" (Luke 15:13). How did he disperse his substance? Above all it is our inborn mind that is our substance and our wealth. As long as we are faithful to the ways of salvation, our mind is at one with itself and with God, the first and highest Mind. Whenever we open the door to the passions, immediately it is dispersed, wandering continually among fleshly and earthly things, all kinds of pleasures and passionate thoughts about them. The wealth of the mind is prudence, which stays with it, discerning between what is better and what is worse, for as long as the mind itself stays obedient to the commandments and counsels of the heavenly Father. Once the mind rebels, prudence is dispersed in fornication and foolishness, shared out between both evils.

You will see the same happening with all our virtues and faculties, which are truly our wealth. Evil is always near at hand, and if they turn aside to it they are dispersed. Our mind itself stretches out in longing towards the one God Who Is, the only Good, the only Desired, the only Bestower of pleasure unmixed with pain. But once the mind has been enfeebled, the soul's ability for real love falls away from what is truly desired, and, scattered among various longings for sensual pleasures, is dispersed, pulled this way and that by desires for superfluous foods, dishonourable bodies, useless objects, and empty, inglorious glory. So the wretched man is cut to pieces and tortured by the cares these things bring, and cannot even enjoy breathing the air or seeing the sun, the riches we all share.

If our mind has not distanced itself from God it stirs up our anger against the devil alone, and puts the soul's courage to use against the evil passions, the rulers of darkness and the spirits of wickedness. But if the mind does not heed the divine commandments of the Lord who armed it with these weapons, it fights against its neighbours, rages against its fellow-countrymen and hunts down those who do not agree with its own absurd desires. Such a man, alas, becomes a murderer. He is not only like an animal, but like a reptile or some venomous creature: a scorpion, a snake, one of the viper's brood, although he was appointed to be a son of God. Do you see how he has dispersed and done away with his substance? "And when", it says, "the younger son had spent all, there arose a mighty famine in that land; and he began to be in want" (Luke 15:14). He did not think yet about returning, profligate as he was, so "he went and joined himself to a citizen of that country; and he sent him into his fields to feed swine" (Luke 15:15).

Who are the citizens and rulers of that country far from God? The demons, of course, by whom the son of the heavenly Father is appointed a brothel-keeper, a chief publican, a captain of thieves and a leader of rebels. The life of pigs, because of its extreme filthiness, is symbolic of all the passions. Those who wallow in the mire of the passions are the pigs, of which the younger son was put in charge, as surpassing them all in self-indulgence. But he could not eat his fill of the husks the pigs ate, meaning that he could not find satisfaction for his desires.

Why is the nature of the body not adequate to serve the impulses of the dissolute man? If someone who loves money gets gold or silver, his need for it grows, and the more it flows in, the more it increases his desire. The whole world might just satisfy one greedy, power-seeking man, but then again, it might not. And as there are many such and only one world, how can even one of them satisfy his desire? So it was that the younger son, who had distanced himself from God, was not able to eat his fill. No one, it says, gave him enough to satisfy him. Who would be able to? God was absent, whom just to regard brings untiring satisfaction to the beholder. As it says, "I shall be satisfied when I have seen your glory" (Ps. 16:15 Lxx). The devil does not want to satisfy shameful desires, because satisfaction naturally produces a change in relation to what is being consumed. It stands to reason therefore that no one gave the younger son enough to satisfy him.

As soon as the son who had broken away from his father came to his senses and realized into what evils he had sunk, he wept over himself saying, "How many hired servants of my father's have bread enough and to spare, and I perish with hunger?" (Luke 15:17). Who are the hired servants? Those who through the sweat of repentance and humility gain salvation as their reward. Sons, by contrast, are those who obey God's commandments out of love. As the Lord said, "If a man love me, he will keep my words" (John 14:23).

So the younger son, who has abandoned his sonship, come out of his holy country of his own free will, and fallen into famine, passes judgment on himself, humbles himself and repents, saying, "I will arise and go to my father, and will say unto him, Father, I have sinned against heaven and before thee" (Luke 15:18). We were right when we said at the beginning that this father is God. How could this son who had left his father have sinned against heaven unless his father was in heaven? For he says, "I have sinned against heaven", meaning against the saints, the citizens of heaven, "and before thee", who dwellest in heaven with Thy saints, "and I am no more worthy to be called thy son: make me as one of thy hired servants" (Luke 15:19). Brought to his senses by humility he is right to say, "make me". Nobody can manage the steps of virtue on his own, though also not without his own deliberate choice. "And he arose", it says, "and came to his father. When he was still a great way off" (Luke 15:20). How did he come to Him when he was still far away, so that his father, having compassion on him, came out to meet him? He who repents in his soul reaches God by his good purpose and his rejection of sin. He is, however, still far from God, tyrannized mentally by habitual sins and failings, and he needs great compassion and help from above if he is to be saved.

The Father of Mercies came down to meet him. He embraced him and ordered his servants, namely the priests, to put on him the best robe, sonship, in which he had been clothed before through holy baptism, and to place a ring on his hand, putting the seal of contemplative virtue on the active part of the soul, as symbolized by the hand, as an earnest of the inheritance to come. He also ordered them to put shoes on his feet as holy protection and assurance to empower him to tread on snakes and scorpions and all the power of the enemy. Then he orders the fatted calf to be brought, slain and offered at table. This calf is the Lord Himself who is led out from the hidden place of divinity, from the heavenly Throne set above all things. Having appeared on earth as a man,

He is slain like a fatted calf for us sinners, that is, He is offered to us as bread to eat.

God shares His joy and celebration over these events with His saints, making our ways His own, and His extreme love for mankind, and saying, "Come, let us eat and be merry" (Luke 15:23). The elder son, however, is angry. Remember the Jews who were angry when the Gentiles were called, the scribes and Pharisees who were scandalized when the Lord accepted sinners and ate with them. Should you wish to think such things even of righteous people, it is not at all strange, if the righteous man is ignorant of the riches of God's goodness which surpass all our understanding. So the father of both sons pleads with the elder one and teaches him what is fitting, saying, "Thou art ever with me", sharing unchanging joy, "It was meet that we should make merry and be glad: for this thy brother was dead, and is alive again; and was lost, and is found" (Luke 15:31, 32). He was dead by reason of sin, and is alive again through repentance. He was lost because he was not to be found in God, but now that he has been found he fills heaven with joy, as it is written, "Joy shall be in heaven over one sinner that repenteth" (Luke 15:7).

Why exactly is the elder son aggrieved? "Thou never gavest me a kid", he says, "that I might make merry with my friends: but as soon as this thy son was come, which hath devoured thy living with harlots, thou hast killed for him the fatted calf" (Luke 15:29–30). God's gifts to us are so surpassingly great that even the angels desire to look into the things He has bestowed upon us through His incarnation, as Peter, the chief apostle, says (1 Pet. 1:12). For this reason righteous people too wanted Christ to come before the appointed time, as Abraham desired to see His day (Matt. 13:17, Luke 10:24, *cf.* John 8:56). But He did not come at that time, and when He did come, He came not to call the righteous but sinners to repentance (Matt. 9:13, Mark 2:17, Luke 5:32), and above all, to be crucified for them, taking away the sin of the world (John 1:29). "For where sin abounded, grace did much more abound" (Rom. 5:20).

That God does not give the righteous even one goat, meaning one sinner, when they ask Him is clear to us for many reasons, but especially on account of the vision of holy and blessed Carpus. When he cursed certain wicked men and said it was unjust that unbelieving men who pervert the straight ways of the Lord should live, not only was he not heard, but he experienced God's displeasure. He heard terrifying words which led him to acknowledge God's unspeakable, incomprehensible forbearance and persuaded him not to curse those living wicked lives but rather to pray for them, as God still grants them time to repent. To show this, and at the same time to prove that He gives great and enviable gifts to those who return to Him in repentance, the God of the penitent, the Father of Mercies, devised this parable.

May we too, brethren, take hold of repentance by our actions. Let us abandon the evil one and his herds. Let us keep away from pigs and the husks they eat, that is to say, the disgusting passions and their devotees. Let us withdraw from evil pastures, namely, habitual sins. Let us flee from the land of the passions, which means unbelief, insatiate desire and intemperance, where there is a terrible famine of good things and where there are passions worse than any famine. Let us run to the immortal Father, the giver of life, as we follow, through the virtues, the path that leads to life. There we shall find that, in His love for mankind, He has come out to meet us, granting us forgiveness of sins, the token of immortality, the earnest of our inheritance to come. As we are taught by the Saviour, as long as the prodigal son was in the land of passions, even though he thought and spoke words of repentance, he gained no benefit at all. Only when he left all his sinful deeds and ran to his father did he attain what was beyond hope. From then on he stayed near him in humility, living chastely and honestly and preserving unharmed the grace renewed in him by God.

May all of us attain this grace and keep it undiminished, that in the age to come we may rejoice with the prodigal son who was saved, in the heavenly Jerusalem, the mother of the living, the Church of the firstborn, in Christ Himself our Lord, to whom be glory for ever. Amen.

On the Parable
Of the Second Coming

LAST SUNDAY, THROUGH THE PARABLE of the prodigal who was saved, the Church commemorated God's incomparable love for mankind. This Sunday it teaches us about His terrifying Judgment to come, following the right order and in accordance with the prophetic sayings: "I will sing of mercy and of judgment" (Ps. 101:1), and, "God hath spoken once; twice have I heard this; that power belongeth unto God. Also unto thee, O Lord, belongeth mercy: for thou renderest to every man according to his works" (Ps. 62:11–12).

Mercy and forbearance precede the divine Judgment. God Himself is the first possessor of every virtue and embraces them all. He is both just and merciful. But as mercy does not go with judgment, as it is written, "Thou shalt not be merciful to a poor man at the judgment" (*cf.* Prov. 24:23), God rightly allotted a proper time to each, appointing the present for forbearance, the future for retribution. The grace of the Spirit so ordered the rites of the Holy Church, that when we learn that we receive forgiveness of sins from what happens here and now, we may press on while still in this present life to attain everlasting mercy and make ourselves worthy of the divine love for mankind. For that Judgment is without mercy for the unmerciful.

We have just recently spoken of God's incomparable compassion towards us. Today our subject is Christ's second coming, the terrifying Judgment, and the things that will then be mysteriously fulfilled, that "eye hath not seen, nor ear heard, neither hath entered into the heart of man" (1 Cor. 2:9), the heart, that is, which has no share in the divine Spirit. These things surpass both the human mind and reason as well as the senses. But although He who teaches us of them is Himself all-knowing and will judge the whole earth, He comes down to his listeners' level and offers words suited to their capability. That is why lightning and clouds, trumpet and throne and the like are brought in, even though we look for new heavens and a new earth (*cf.* 2 Pet. 3:13), in accordance with His own promise, for all that now exists will be changed.

If mere words, words adapted to our measure, can fill the soul of the prudent listener with trembling and awe, who will withstand when the reality is accomplished? What sort of lives ought we to be living in holiness and godliness, as we wait for the coming of the Day of God, that day on which, as the divine Peter says, "the heavens being on fire shall be dissolved, and the elements shall melt with fervent heat?" (2 Pet. 3:12). Before that, however, will be the grievous coming of the Antichrist to oppose and threaten the faith which, if it were not shortened, being allowed only for a brief time, there should no flesh be saved, as the Lord says in the Gospels (Matt. 24:22, Mark 13:20). So He exhorts his followers, "Watch ye therefore, and pray always, that ye may be accounted worthy to escape all these things that shall come to pass, and to stand before the Son of man" (Luke 21:36).

All these things are full of overwhelming horror, but worse still than these are threatened for those who waste their lives in unbelief, injustice and laziness. As the Lord says Himself, "Then shall all the tribes of the earth mourn" (Matt. 24:30). The tribes of the earth are people who do not obey Him who came down from heaven, who neither know the heavenly Father nor call upon Him, and do not lift up their race to Him by deeds that resemble His own. Again the Lord says, "For as a snare shall it come on all them that dwell on the face of the whole earth" (Luke 21:35, Isa. 24:17 Lxx), meaning those nailed to the earth and earthly concerns by dissipation, drunkenness, self-indulgence and the cares of this life, wholly taken up with outwardly visible splendour, riches, glory and pleasure. The expression "face of the earth" refers to the earth's apparent pleasantness, whereas by saying "them that dwell" He implies their continuing inward attachment. With these words he puts sinners who continue unrepentant to the end together with the godless, for as Isaiah foretold, "The lawless and the sinners shall burn together, and none shall quench them" (Isa. 1:31 Lxx). "But our commonwealth is in heaven", says the apostle, "from whence also we look for the Saviour" (Phil. 3:20). The Lord said to His disciples, "you are not of the world" (John 15:19), and also, "When these things begin to come to pass, then look up and lift up your heads, for your redemption draweth nigh" (Luke 21:28).

Notice how those who live according to Christ are filled with ineffable joy and courage by the events immediately following these, while those who live according to the flesh are filled with shame, suffering and dejection. As Paul too proclaims, "God will render to every man according to his deeds: to them who by patient continuance in well doing seek for glory and honour and immortality, eternal life: but unto them that obey evil, indignation, and wrath, tribulation and anguish upon every soul of man that doeth evil" (Rom. 2:6–9). In the days of Noah, when evil had increased and held sway over nearly all the human race, there was a flood sent by God which wiped out everything living and kept safe only the righteous man and his family to start another world (cf. Gen. 6:5–9:2). And after that God again cut off evil when it was rampant, in turn burning the Sodomites to ashes (cf. Gen. 19:1–28), drowning Pharaoh's men in the sea in an extraordinary way (cf. Exod. 14:19–31), and destroying the shameless race of the Jews by famine, revolt, disease and bitter retribution (cf. Exod. 16:1–3; 17: 1–4; 32:1ff).

Our Physician made use of harsh medicines and remedies for our sake, but nevertheless He did not disregard such as work pleasantly and agreeably. He raised up fathers, revealed prophets, performed signs, gave the law and appointed angels. Since these means were powerless against the irrepressible impetus of our wickedness, the Word of God Himself, the great Remedy for grave sins, bowed the heavens and came down. Having become like us in everything, though without sin (*cf.* Heb. 4:15), He abolished sin in Himself. By giving us strength He dulled its sting, and on the Cross He put to shame its rulers and fellow-workers, that through death He might destroy him that had the power of death (Heb. 2:14).

As in the days of Noah He flooded sinners with water, later He flooded sin with His own righteousness and grace, and raised Himself immortal, as a seed and first fruit of the world without end, a sign and proof of the resurrection for which we truly hope. When He had risen and ascended He sent out apostles into all the inhabited world, presented us with an innumerable throng of martyrs, appointed a multitude of teachers, and revealed companies of saints. Then when He had done everything, and omitted nothing that had to be, He saw the evil caused by the independence of our free will once more brought to a head. Or rather, in those days it will be seen to have reached such a peak that people will worship and obey the Antichrist, abandoning the true God and His true Christ. Then He will come again from heaven with great power and glory (*cf.* Mark 13:26), no longer to be patient but to punish those who in the days of his forbearance heaped up wrath against themselves. He will cut off the incurable from the healthy like rotting limbs and deliver them into the fire, but His own He will rescue from the spiteful abuse of evil men and from contact with them, and will make them heirs of the kingdom of heaven.

Immediately after the abominable advent of the Antichrist, He who fashioned everything will shake it all again. As the prophet says, "Yet once more I shake not the earth only, but also heaven" (Heb. 12:26, *cf.* Hag. 2:21). Straight away He shakes the world, dismantles the upper boundary of the universe, folds up the vault of heaven, mingles the earth with fire and puts everything into confusion. From below He forces open the foundations of the whole world, from above He sends down the multitude of stars like an indescribably terrible hurricane upon the heads of those who made the evil one their God, that the believers in the Antichrist might be punished first by this means, whose minds were engrossed in him and who were persuaded that the opposite to God was God.

Then He will appear in unutterable glory and, as He once breathed life into our first father Adam, so with a clear trumpet call He will bring everyone to life. He will have the dead from all ages standing before Him alive. But He will not bring the godless to judgment nor count them worthy of a word. For according to the Scriptures the ungodly will be resurrected not for judgment but for condemnation (*cf.* Matt. 12:41–42, Luke 11:31–32).

He will subject all our affairs to judgment, as we read in today's Gospel. "When the Son of man", it says, "shall come in his glory, and all the holy angels with him" (Matt. 25:31). At His first coming the glory of His divinity was hidden beneath the flesh which He took from us and for our sake. Now it is hidden, together with the flesh which is divine, with the Father in heaven. But then He will reveal all His glory, for He will appear in radiance from the east to the west, illuminating the ends of the earth with the rays of His Godhead, while the trumpet that brings the dead to life shall sound throughout the world, summoning everything to Him. He also brought angels with Him before, though invisibly, and He restrained their zeal against God's enemies. Afterwards He will lead them openly and will not keep silent, but will put the disobedient to shame and hand them over for punishment.

"When the Son of man shall come in his glory, and all the holy angels with him, then", it says, "shall he sit upon the throne of his glory" (Matt. 25:31). Daniel foresaw and foretold this, saying, "Behold thrones were set and the Ancient of days did sit, and I beheld one like the Son of man came with the clouds of heaven, and came to the Ancient of days. And there was given him all honour and dominion. Thousand thousands ministered unto him, and ten thousand times ten thousand stood before him" (*cf.* Dan. 7:9–13). The Holy Gospel says, in accordance with this, that in those days, "before him shall be gathered all nations: and he shall separate them one from another, as a shepherd divideth the sheep from the goats" (Matt. 25:32). He calls the righteous sheep because they are meek and gentle, walk the level path of the virtues that He trod, and are like Him. For He was Himself called a lamb by the Forerunner and Baptist who said, "Behold the Lamb of God, which taketh away the sin of the world" (John 1:29). The sinners He calls goats because they are audacious and unruly, and rush down the precipices of sin. The sheep, it says, He shall set on his right hand as those who act rightly, but the others on the left. "Then", it says, "shall the king say", without adding which king or of whom he is king, for there is no other, but only one is Lord, one is King, He who by nature is Lord of all. Then the one and only King will say to those on His right hand, "Come, ye blessed of my Father, inherit the kingdom prepared for you from the foundation of the world" (Matt. 25:34).

The world was founded with this in view from the beginning. The heavenly, pre-eternal Counsel of the Father, according to which the Angel of the Father's Great Counsel made man (Isa. 9:6) as a living creature in His own likeness as well as His image, was for this end: to enable man at some time to contain the greatness of God's kingdom, the blessedness of God's inheritance and the perfection of the heavenly Father's blessing, by which everything visible and invisible was made. He did not refer to "the visible world" but to "the world" without qualification, heavenly as well as earthly. Even the indescribable divine self-emptying, the theandric way of life, the saving passion, all the sacraments were planned beforehand in God's providence and wisdom for this end, that everyone who is shown to be faithful in the present shall hear the Saviour say, "Well done, thou good servant: thou hast been faithful over a few things: enter thou into the joy of thy Lord" (Matt. 25:21). "Come", He says, "you who made good use of the earthly, perishable and fleeting world in accordance with my will, and inherit as well the lasting, heavenly world which is now at hand." "For I was an hungered, and ye gave me meat: I was thirsty, and ye gave me drink: I was a stranger, and ye took me in: naked, and ye clothed me: I was sick, and ye visited me: I was in prison, and ye came unto me" (Matt. 25:35–36).

At this point we might enquire why He only mentions works of mercy, and why it is only on account of them that He gives this blessing, inheritance and kingdom. But if we listen with understanding, He does not mention these alone. Earlier He called those who performed works of mercy sheep, and in this way

He bears witness to their likeness to Himself, their possession of every virtue, and their readiness to die for the sake of what is good. Just as He was led as a sheep to the slaughter, and like a lamb dumb before his shearer, according to the Scriptures (Isa. 53:7, Acts 8:32).

Because they are people like this, he extols their good works as well. Anyone who is to inherit the everlasting kingdom must have good works as the proof and the fruit of love, as the crown of all the other virtues. The Lord showed this in the parable of the Ten Virgins (Matt. 25:1–13). Not everyone who happens to be there is led into the bridechamber, only those adorned with virginity, which cannot be accomplished without ascetic effort, self-control and many different struggles in the cause of virtue. Besides they must hold lamps in their hands, which denotes their minds and the watchful knowledge enclosed within, borne upon and supported by the practical part of their souls – as signified by their hands. Such knowledge must be dedicated to God for life and set alight with His brilliance. But oil in abundance is needed to keep the lamps burning, and this oil is love, the summit of all the virtues. If you lay down foundations and build walls, but do not put on the roof, you leave it all useless. In the same way, if you acquire every virtue except love, they are all useless and senseless. Though the roof cannot be constructed without the supporting walls.

The Lord therefore grants His inheritance to those who have sealed the other virtues with loving deeds, who either ascended to love by way of a blameless life or fled to it for refuge through repentance. Those who have kept safe the mystical rebirth that comes from God, I call sons, whereas the hired servants have been called back again to grace as a reward for many different labours of repentance and humility.

After having initially expounded various matters concerning the Judgment in the Holy Gospels, He introduces the subject of love, which fulfills and stirs up the virtues previously enumerated. But the righteous will reply (Matt. 25:37–39): "Lord, when saw we thee an hungred, and fed thee? or thirsty, and gave thee drink? When saw we thee a stranger, and took thee in? or naked, and clothed thee? Or when saw we thee sick, or in prison, and came unto thee?" Do you see that those on the right are also called righteous? Accordingly their mercy proceeds from, and is accompanied by, righteousness. Do you see that testimony is given that the righteous also possess another virtue, humility, in the fullness of their love, like a protective wall raised up around them at the right moment? They insist that they are unworthy of the proclamation and the praise, as having done nothing good, although it is attested that they left no good undone.

I think this is why the Lord responds to them boldly, that they may clearly show what they are like, and may be lifted up by humility and rightly find grace with Him who bestows it abundantly on the humble, for "God resisteth the proud, but giveth grace unto the humble" (Prov. 3:34 Lxx, Jas. 4:6). He now tells them, "Verily I say unto you, Inasmuch as ye have done it unto one of the least of these my brethren, ye have done it unto me" (Matt. 25:40). He calls the person least on account of his poverty and lowliness, but His brother because He Himself lived in this way on earth according to the flesh.

Listen and be glad, all you who are poor and needy, for in this you are God's brethren. Even if you are poor and lowly against your will, with patience and thanksgiving voluntarily turn it to your own good. Listen, all you who are rich, and long for blessed poverty, that you may become more truly heirs and brethren of Christ than those who are involuntarily poor, for of His own free will He made Himself poor for our sake. Listen and groan, all you who overlook your suffering brethren, or rather, Christ's brethren, and do not give the poor a share of your abundant food, shelter, clothing and care as appropriate, nor offer your surplus to meet their need. Let us listen and groan ourselves, for I who am telling you these things stand accused by my conscience of not being completely free of this passion. While many people shiver and go without, I am well fed and clothed. But more grievously to be mourned over are those who have treasures in excess of their daily needs, who hold on to them and even strive to increase them. They have been commanded to love their neighbours as themselves and have not even loved them as dust, for what are gold and silver, which they loved more than their brethren, other than dust.

But let us change direction, repent and agree together to supply the needs of the poor brethren among us by whatever means we have. If we prefer not to empty out all we possess for the love of God, let us at least not callously hold on to everything for ourselves. Let us do something, then humble ourselves before God and obtain forgiveness from Him for what we have failed to do. For His love for mankind makes up for our omissions, that we may never hear the horrifying voice: "Then shall he say also unto them on the left hand, Depart from me, ye cursed" (Matt. 25:41). How great a horror! "Be ye removed from life, cast out of paradise, deprived of light!"

Not this alone, but also, "Depart from me, ye cursed, unto everlasting fire, prepared for the devil and his angels" (Matt. 25:41). Those on the right will have life and have it more abundantly: life through being with God, abundance of life through continuing as sons and heirs of His kingdom. Those of the left, having failed to gain the kingdom by being far away from God, will find even more evil through being ranked with the demons, and delivered up to the punishing fire.

What sort of fire is that, which burns bodies, and rational beings with bodies, and spirits without bodies, tormenting them while detaining them for ever alive? It will melt even the fiery element in us, for the Scripture says "the elements shall melt with fervent heat" (2 Pet. 3:10, 12). How greatly is suffering increased when there is no hope of redemption. And that fire is unquenchable. Again, what gives it its violent impetus? They say a river draws that fire along, apparently bearing it ever further away from God. So He did not say "You have departed", but "Depart from me, ye cursed". "You have long been cursed by the poor, and as they suffered so much you deserve cursing. 'Depart', He tells them, 'into everlasting fire, prepared', not for you, 'but for the devil and his angels'. For this was not originally My will. I did not create you for this, nor did I prepare the fire for you. The unquenchable fire was lit for the demons who are irreversibly in the grip of evil. You joined them because your unrepentant minds were like theirs, and you share the dwelling of the evil angels by your own choice." "For I was an hungred, and ye gave me no meat; I was thirsty, and you gave me no drink: I was a stranger, and ye took me not in: naked and ye clothed me not: sick, and in prison, and ye visited me not" (Matt. 25:42–43). As love and loving deeds, brethren, are the fulfilment of the virtues, so hatred and the outcome of hatred, behaviour devoid of compassion and a mind devoid of the desire to share, are the full measure of sin. As the virtues follow upon benevolence and are associated with it, so evil deeds follow upon hatred for our fellow man, and for this hatred alone they are condemned.

I wanted to say that there was no greater proof of hatred than preferring excess money to our brother. But I see that evil has found a greater proof of hatred for our fellow man. For some people not only do not give alms out of their abundance, but even appropriate what belongs to others. Let them deduce from the sentence given to the unmerciful what their own fate and suffering will be, and how indescribable and unbearable is the condemnation they deserve. Let them give up injustice and by works of repentance find mercy with God. On that day the unmerciful will reply, "Lord, when saw we thee an hungred, or athirst, or a stranger, or naked, or sick, or in prison, and did not minister unto thee?" (Matt. 25:44).

Observe this last evil: pride is yoked with callous behaviour, as humility is with compassion. When the righteous are praised for doing good they humble themselves the more, without justifying themselves. When these others are accused of being devoid of compassion by Him who cannot lie, they do not humbly throw themselves to the ground, but answer back and justify themselves. So they go on to hear, "Verily I say unto you, Inasmuch as ye did it not to one of the least of these, ye did it not to me." So "these shall go away", it says, "into everlasting punishment: but the righteous into life eternal" (Matt. 25:46).

Let us be merciful to ourselves by being merciful to others, gain compassion by showing compassion, and do good that good may be done to us. For we receive the like in return: good works, benevolence, love, mercy and compassion, but not merely to the same value and measure of excellence. You give out of what you possess as a man, and only as much as a man can bestow. But you receive in return a hundredfold from the inexhaustible divine treasures, together with eternal life, and benefit from as many great bounties as God can bestow, which "eye hath not seen, nor ear heard, neither have entered into the heart of man" (1 Cor. 2:9).

May we make haste to obtain the riches of kindness and buy an eternal kingdom in exchange for a little money. We should be afraid even now of the sentence pronounced on the unmerciful, lest we receive the same condemnation. There is no need to fear that if we give alms we shall become poor, for we shall hear Christ say, "Come, ye blessed of my Father, inherit the kingdom" (Matt. 25:34). Let us be afraid of being shown to be excluded from loving God by our lack of compassion, and do everything to avoid this. "For he that loveth not his brother whom he hath seen", says the evangelist, "how can he love God whom he hath not seen" (1 John 4:20). And how can someone who does not love God be with Him? Anyone who is not with Him will be driven away from Him, and anyone driven away from Him will certainly fall into hell.

Let us show loving deeds towards our brethren in Christ by being merciful to the poor and restoring those who have gone astray, whatever their poverty or error may be, by obtaining justice for the wronged, by encouraging those laid low by sickness, whether their suffering be due to visible enemies and physical ailments or to invisible evil spirits and dishonourable passions, by visiting those confined in prison, and even by bearing with those who injure us, forgiving one another any cause for complaint we may have among ourselves, as Christ forgave us. In a word, let us show love to one another by all our actions and words. So may we attain to God's love, receive His blessing and inherit the eternal heavenly kingdom promised to us and prepared for us from the foundation of the world.

May we all attain to this by the grace and love for mankind of our Lord Jesus Christ, to whom, together with the Father and also the Holy Spirit, be honour and glory unto the ages of ages. Amen.

On the Parable of the Unforgiving Servant

WHEN GOD FORMED MAN WITH FREE WILL, He deigned to make careful provision for him so that, by using his freedom rightly, he would incline not towards evil, but towards the good. From the very beginning He made him in His own image and likeness (Gen. 1:26), that looking towards his good archetype, man might not fall away from goodness, and God might thereafter justly show him, as His own image, the riches of His kindness to a greater extent than He would to the rest of His creatures. Thus would He draw man more and more towards goodness commensurate and compatible with His own. It is possible for man, by imitating His Creator, to be good in His image, though no one can equal God in goodness.

Observe how many great gifts God has bestowed on us, and that He presents Himself to us as an example of active kindness. I shall pass over for the present those natural benefits which He has given us from birth. Looking just at these, David said to God, "Such knowledge is too wonderful for me; it is high, I cannot attain to it" (Ps. 139:6). I shall, however, briefly mention those gifts which surround us from without. All things visible and invisible God made for man's sake. Nor was it just the heavens, the earth, water, air, fire, and everything they contain, and all the species of animals and plants, which we cannot enumerate in detail, that He made for man, but also the multitude of different kinds of angels (*cf.* Col. 1:16), some of whom He appointed to guide the world and lead the nations, as God's prophets, who learnt these things from Him, tell us (Dan. 10:13), and others, to be ministers for the sake of those who are to inherit eternal salvation, as the great Paul, who also was taught by God, revealed to us (Heb. 1:14). But why speak only of His creatures? For our sake He made Himself man. What speech can express the words He Himself uttered for us, His way of life, the virtues He taught us, the greatness of the miracles which He did for us? By far the greatest miracle of all was that He gave Himself over to death for our sake, rose again and ascended for us, He who, as God, lives and has His Being eternally in heaven, and is everywhere and above all, who was before all ages and continues throughout all ages and beyond.

Mercy was the source of all He did for us. What else but love for mankind, charity and mercy moved Him to bestow such great benefits upon us? There are two aspects of this mercy. Before we sinned against Him, He mercifully made up for what was deficient in our nature with His many bounties. Then after we transgressed, He was not only constantly forbearing, but in His abundant compassion He continually gave us more and better gifts and led us onwards. He did not requite evil for evil, nor did He just give good for evil, but the most excellent of good things, greater and nobler than all else. Afterwards, He gave Himself for our sake, which of all goods is the first, and greatest, and most excellent, or rather that which is uniquely good and beyond compare.

Mercy is therefore a twofold virtue. On the one hand, it means giving shelter, protection, food, and necessary aid to those in want. On the other, it is patience, forgiveness of wrongs, and compassion towards those who offend. When the Son of God became man for our sake and deigned to be our teacher, He led us towards the first kind of mercy, which consists of sharing our possessions, by saying, "Give to him that asketh thee, and from him that would borrow of thee turn not thou away" (Matt. 5:42), and, "Lay up for yourselves treasures in heaven, where neither moth nor rust doth corrupt, and where thieves do not break through nor steal" (Matt. 6:20), and again elsewhere, "Give alms of such things as ye have; and, behold, all things are clean unto you" (Luke 11:41).

Urging us to give to others, not just by these words but also with a parable, He brings before our eyes that terrible future advent, and shows us Himself as King sitting upon His throne of glory (Matt. 25:31–46). He sets those who have been generous on His right hand, as they have acted rightly. The rest He sets on His left, reproaches them for not giving, calls them cursed, as though by failing to help the needy they had shown unkindness to Him Himself, and dispatches them into the everlasting fire prepared for the devil and his angels. As for those who have been generous, He praises them openly, and accepts their benevolence to the poor as if it had been offered to Himself. He bears witness that they have His Father's blessing, and makes them heirs of the kingdom prepared for them from the foundation of the world. By making such statements in the Gospels the Lord urges us towards one type of mercy, giving alms to those in need.

But what does He say about mercy's other aspect, forbearance and compassion towards those who have wronged us? "Recompense no man evil for evil" (Rom. 12:17), but "overcome evil with good" (Rom. 12:21). "Condemn not, and ye shall not be condemned" (Luke 6:37). And, "If ye forgive men their trespasses, your heavenly Father will also forgive you: but if ye forgive not men their trespasses, neither will your Father which is in heaven forgive your trespasses" (cf. Matt. 6:14–15). As in the case of the first type of mercy, He used words of exhortation and also spurred us on by means of what would happen when He sat before us as Shepherd and King, so in the case of forgiveness of wrongs and compassion He not only spoke the words to which we have referred, but also went on to give us a parable, which was read to you today from the Gospel, saying, "The kingdom of heaven is likened unto a certain king, which would take account of his servants. And when he had begun to reckon, one was brought unto him, which owed him ten thousand talents" (Matt. 18:23–24).

He is here referring to His Father as a man who is a king, just as He refers to Himself as such when He speaks of the end of the world (Matt. 13:40–41; and 16:28). Although the Father is likened to a human being, this is only by way of a parable. Christ Himself, however, was not just likened to a man in a parable, but was actually made man like us. Of course, the Son and the Father have the same throne and the same kingdom, but since, in His words about doing good to our neighbour, the Lord said, "I was an hungered", "I was thirsty", and so on, and called the destitute His brethren (*cf.* Matt. 25:35–40), in addition to making other allusions to His Incarnation, that is why He speaks of Himself there as the King sitting before us. And by referring to sheep and goats in that parable, He set Himself before us as King and Shepherd. Here, by contrast, as He makes mention of servants, accounts, and money from the royal treasury, He is speaking of His Father sitting before us, balancing accounts and calling in debts.

Why is it that the first passage says the king shall sit, the nations shall be gathered, He shall separate them and shall speak, with everything in the future tense (Matt. 25:31–46), whereas here the kingdom is likened to a king who wanted to settle accounts, the debtor was brought, and the Lord gave orders, with all the words referring to the past (Matt. 18:23–35)? Because those things related in the former parable belong to the age to come, whereas most of the events in this one take place here and now. When the man owing ten thousand talents was brought before the king, without being able to pay, "His Lord", it says, "commanded him to be sold, and his wife, and children, and all that he had, and payment to be made" (Matt. 18:25). But when he fell down, asked him to have patience and promised to pay, the Lord was moved with compassion, released him and forgave him the debt. In the age to come there will be no such thing as postponement, promises from the debtor, settlement of debts, or any sort of forgiveness from the giver of all, who will demand an account of all.

Even the fact that the man owing ten thousand talents was brought when the king began balancing accounts is not compatible with the age to come. Then all things will come to an end, whereas here they are just beginning. The subsequent events in the parable also belong to the present. "But the same servant went out", it says, "and found one of his fellowservants, which owed him an hundred pence: and he laid hands on him, and took him by the throat, saying, Pay me that thou owest" (Matt. 18:28). And when the fellow-servant fell down before him, pleading with him and promising to pay, he was not in the least merciful, but went and threw him into prison, until he should pay all he owed. What way out will there be when that time comes? What debts will then be owed to fellow-servants? Will payment be demanded or attacks made? "And his fellowservant", it says, "fell down at his feet, and besought him, saying, Have patience with me, and I will pay thee all. And he would not: but went and cast him into prison till he should pay the debt" (Matt. 18:29–30). In the age to come we shall not suffer violence from one another, nor shall we fall down one before the other with entreaties. For then there will be one before whom "every knee shall bow, of things in heaven and things in earth, and things under the earth" (*cf.* Phil. 2:10). But the other fellow-servants, it says, were very sorry on account of the man's heartlessness to his fellow-servant, and told their lord all that had happened. He angrily accused the pitiless servant, and handed him over to the tormentors, until he should pay all that he owed (Matt. 18:31–34).

Although you could see this final incident as happening in the present, it belongs more to the future. Then the accusation will be public, the sentence without mercy and the torture neverending: "till", it says, "he should pay all that was due to him". It is absolutely impossible for payment equivalent to our debts towards God to be obtained from us. So "till he should pay all" means he was tormented for ever. But how do all the earlier elements in the parable take place here and now: the king's court, the accusation of debtors, the subsequent demand for repayment and condemnation, then forgiveness, followed by condemnation once more, and all the rest? This church of God is like another heaven within the holy veil (*cf.* Heb. 6:19; 9:3ff), which, like the tabernacles beyond the heavens, holds the royal throne on which the King of all sits and invisibly settles His accounts with His servants, all of us who stand round about and pray.

Many, myself included, are reproached by God through the words we hear sung and read in this place, because we have not put these ten thousand (*cf.* Matt. 18:24), meaning this large number of words, to good use, each of which is a talent, as it carries a great and heavy punishment. Cain apparently committed one sin by killing his brother, but according to Scripture, vengeance was taken on him sevenfold, that is to say, many times (*cf.* Gen. 4:15). We are not just accused of being in debt, but learn from the divine words about the punishments stored up for the guilty. When we hear of these matters, for as long as we remain in church, we repent, prostrate ourselves, make entreaties, promise to live as pleases God from now on, and even obtain forgiveness, when we have stayed here until the end in fervent supplication. As the Scripture says, "Turn ye unto me, saith the Lord of hosts, and I will turn unto you" (Zech. 1:3), and "I will remember your sin no more" (*cf.* Jer. 31:34).

Afterwards, when we come out of church and meet people who have wronged us, who sometimes fall down before us and beseech us, we are severe, merciless and implacable towards them, even though their sins towards us are not worth a penny in comparison with our own sins against God, which are measured in huge numbers of talents. The Lord pitied us when we repented, and forgave us much, but when He sees how heartless and unyielding we are to our fellows, His wrath is justly kindled against us, and He delivers us up to unendurable torments, both temptations here, and unending future punishments, in accordance with the words of the Truth Himself. "So likewise", says the Lord, "shall my heavenly Father do also unto you, if ye from your hearts forgive not every one his brother their trespasses" (Matt. 18:35). What is even more terrible is that we shall find, alas, that God's true servants, the holy angels and the saints, whom we hope by our prayers here to have as ambassadors and intercessors to God on our behalf, will be inciting Him against us, if in this present life we fail to show compassion to those who offend against us. This is because the holy angels and saints are those whom, as we learned earlier, with great sorrow denounce to the Lord our hard and merciless frame of mind. We were correct in saying at the outset that the king and judge of whom the Lord speaks in this parable is His Father. For He does not say here that He Himself will deliver the cruel man to the tormentors, but that His heavenly Father will do so.

Brethren, let us be afraid of the zeal of the saints against us on that day. Let us tremble at the divine sentence, and respect God's earlier patience towards us. Let us reckon up how much we owe God, compared with other people's debts towards us. "How oft", Peter asked the Lord, "shall my brother sin against me, and I forgive him? till seven times?" And he heard in reply, "I say not unto thee, Until seven times: but, Until seventy times seven" (Matt. 18:21–22), although it is almost impossible for our brother to wrong us so often. But each of us has sinned more frequently than that against God. If you look carefully at how great one sin is, bearing in mind against whom it is committed, you will find it incomparably worse than all your brother's sins, be they seventy times seven.

Seeing that you owe so many weighty talents to God, and as soon as you asked Him to be patient, your debt was written off, if you are then asked by a fellow-servant to be forbearing over a small debt of silver coins (which is what "pence" means), will you not eagerly comply? Otherwise the whole amount will be rightly demanded from you. How can it be unjust for you to suffer the loss of everything as well as receiving condemnation for your ingratitude? For that reason one of the prophets says, "As thou hast done, so shall it be done unto thee: thy reward shall return upon thine own head" (Obad. 15). Let us not, brethren, wait for God's accusation, wrath and judgment, but let us put on, as the apostle says, "bowels of mercies" (Col. 3:12). By showing compassion in our words and deeds, let us, as the same apostle teaches, "be kind one to another, tenderhearted, forgiving one another", if we have a complaint against anyone, "even as God for Christ's sake hath forgiven you" (Eph. 4:32). In this way, the grace of Christ will surely be with us, and will, moreover, be an earnest of the unspeakable promise to come.

The man who wrongs us causes us so many benefits, if we are willing, that I regard him as a richly laden merchant-ship easily capable of paying off our debt of ten thousand talents and of guaranteeing future riches. I inwardly perceive him as the spiritual equivalent of what we recently witnessed with our own eyes in this city. The barbarians attacked, besieged the town, and cut off vital supplies from inland, posing the grave threat that they would conquer us through lack of essential provisions. But then a vessel laden with many tons of wheat appeared and landed in our harbours, making the barbarians' threat ineffectual, lowering the price of food, and also providing us with a store of necessary supplies for the future.

In the same way, the spiritual enemy of all Christian people, who is far more savage than any barbarian, invisibly attacks us. He cuts off the soul on all sides from everything it needs for salvation, surrounds it with a dearth of virtue, crushes it with despair because of its lack of good deeds, and so conquers and destroys it. Then, obviously, by the providence of the Saviour of sinners, someone comes along who has wronged us and needs our compassion, and when he has received it from us, he makes all the devil's malice against us of no effect, reconciles us with God, offers us abundant supplies of mercy and salvation, and gives us a promise of eternal life.

May we all attain to this through the grace and love for mankind of our Lord Jesus Christ, to whom belong all glory, power, honour and worship, together with His Father without beginning and His all-holy, good and life-giving Spirit, now and for ever and unto the ages of ages. Amen.

On the Parable of the Marriage Feast

I SHALL START by quoting to your charity the end of the Lord's parable in today's Gospel reading, "Many are called, but few are chosen" (Matt. 22:14). The Lord teaches us this through the whole parable, that we might strive to be not merely among those invited, but among the elect. For anyone who is just one of those called, but not one of the chosen, is not only deprived of the light without evening, but is also led away into outer darkness. After his hands have been bound, because they did not do God's work, and his feet, because they did not run towards God, he is delivered up to weeping and gnashing of teeth (Matt. 22:13).

First of all, you might be puzzled why the Lord said that many, but not all, were called. If not everyone was invited, then it is unjust that those who were not should forfeit the promised good things, and experience the threatened torments. Perhaps if they had been called, they might have obeyed. But whereas it is reasonable to suppose that, if they had not been called, it would be unfair for them to be rejected, it is untrue that not everyone was called. When the Lord was carried up to heaven after His resurrection from the dead, He said to His disciples, "Go ye into all the world, and preach the gospel to every creature" (Mark 16:15), and, "Make disciples of all nations, baptizing them in the name of the Father, and of the Son, and of the Holy Ghost: teaching them to observe all things whatsoever I have commanded you" (Matt. 28:19–20). The fact that the disciples put this command into action is adequately proved by the great Paul. "Have they not heard?" he asks, "Yes, verily, their sound went into all the earth, and their words to the ends of the world", referring to the apostles' preaching (Rom. 10:18). So all were summoned, and those who did not come to the faith, shall justly be punished. Why, therefore, did the Lord say that many were called, but not all? Because at this point He was speaking about those who had come to Christ, which is why He put this statement later, after the parable. If, when someone was invited, he were to obey the summons, and, having been baptized, were to be called by Christ's name, but were not to behave in a way worthy of his calling, nor fulfil the promises made at his baptism to live according to Christ, then, although he was called, he was not chosen.

But some people are surprised at this as well, or rather, being earth and clay, and born yesterday, they accuse Him who dwells from all eternity above the heavens. Why, they ask, did God call those whom He knew would not obey Him at all, or at least not in their actions? In short, why did He make men who would be damned, when He foreknew what would happen? Instead of listening to the Lord's words, "As the heavens are higher than the earth, so are my thoughts higher than your thoughts" (Isa. 55:9), they rebuke and call to account God, who is beyond our mind's grasp. Are we any different from ants? Are our bodies not made of the same stuff as theirs? Do we not eat the same food, live in the same places, and have the use of more or less the same faculties? In fact, some of the ants' abilities are better than our own: they see more clearly what will be beneficial to them in the future, they are much better at knowing what they will need, and are more diligent about the annual harvest. Even so, are we not more excellent than they by virtue of our rational souls? Then again, what is that superiority compared with God's superiority over us?

If all the ants in the world put together could never comprehend our most insignificant deed or thought, as we are superior to them in every respect, how are we able to understand the works and mind of God, who is infinitely superior to us, or to make accurate conjectures about the sequence of events, without faith? As the great luminary in the heavens could not give us daylight, if its brilliance did not surpass our vision, so God, who created our human nature, could not provide us with salvation, if He were comprehensible to us, and His wisdom and goodness did not go beyond our understanding.

As for those who accuse God of calling people who were not going to act in obedience to Him, no doubt they would also have held Him responsible for the destruction of such people, had He not called them. He called them so that no one could say that He was the cause of their being punished. Why was it, then, that He created men who were to be damned? He did not make them to be punished, but to be saved, as is clear from the fact that He called them. If He had wanted to damn anyone at all, He would not have called everyone to salvation. If God led me and called me to salvation through His goodness, but I turned out evil, ought my wickedness, before it even existed, to have overcome His eternal goodness and have thwarted it? That would be totally unreasonable. People who assert otherwise and make accusations against the Creator are actually saying that it was wrong to make human beings rational. For reason would be pointless without free choice and the power of self-governance. How can someone have the freedom to choose and the power to act freely, unless he were able to be evil, should he so wish? If he could not be wicked, nor could he, presumably, be good.

Anyone who states that God should not have made those people who will be punished, is also saying that He should not have made those who will be saved, or any rational and free beings at all. As everything else was made for the sake of mankind, such a person is contending that God should not have created anything. Do you see the absurdity of this? God made the human race rational and free, and because of men's tendency to please themselves and the different uses to which they put their freedom, some were to become bad, and others good. What should God, who is truly good, have done? Ought He not to have brought good men into being on account of those who would turn out evil? That would be the greatest injustice imaginable. For even if there were only going to be one good person, it would not have been just to stop creating, since one man who does God's will is superior to innumerable sinners. Should we perhaps tell those who pick out gold from the dirt, that they should not start by collecting the useless earth along with the gold dust? We would hear in reply, that if they did not do so, they could not select out the gold. In the same way, there would be no elect if the others were not called as well, and how could they be called if they had not been made?

Let us bring our arguments closer to the point, and ask those who lay charges against the one who wishes all to be saved, about people who do not want their own salvation. As we are all mortal, we need nourishment. But as our body's natural processes select and absorb part of our food for our sustenance and, having made what remains ill-smelling, get rid of it as useless by the appropriate means, does this mean that you would completely reject food on account of that part of it which will end up as dung? Or will you accept food in its entirety on account of that portion of it which is chosen, assimilated and incorporated, through our digestive system, for our physical sustenance? There is obviously no need for a reply. We provide the answer by our actions, as we feed ourselves every day, consuming food that is unsuitable for our physical nourishment for the sake of that which is. What makes us do this? Our inborn desire to live. Similarly, because of His innate kindness and love of goodness, God did not stop bringing good people into being on account of those who would become bad by their own fault. Rather, He created those who would be evil for the sake of the good.

Have you not seen how doctors do not allow patients to go without food when, because of the weakness of their stomach, they cannot keep down nourishment but vomit it up? Why do they urge them to eat? Because their constitution receives something, however little, from the food, even though most of what they eat is rendered useless by the vomiting. That is why the art of medicine is rightly called philanthropic. So God's love for what is good and His philanthropy are demonstrated above all by this: that although those who seek their own salvation are few, in comparison with the great number of those who will not be saved, yet He created the whole human race, and although not many are going to be chosen, in His exceedingly great love for mankind He called everyone.

"The kingdom of heaven", it says, "is like unto a certain king, which made a marriage for his son, and sent forth his servants to call them that were bidden to the wedding: and they would not come" (Matt. 22:2–3). The wedding here means the union of the Son of God with man's nature, and hence with our Church. Similarly, when Paul says that marriage is a great mystery, he adds, "But I speak concerning Christ and the church" (Eph. 5:32). Again, he tells us elsewhere, "I have espoused you to one husband, that I may present you as a chaste virgin to Christ" (2 Cor. 11:2). Why does the original not say that the King of heaven made a marriage for his son, but use the word "nuptials", in the plural? Because whenever Christ, the bridegroom of pure souls, is mystically united with each soul, He gives the Father occasion to rejoice over this as at a wedding. It is Christ Himself who says, "Joy shall be in heaven over one sinner that repenteth" (Luke 15:7). For joy, according to the apostle, is the fruit of the Holy Spirit (Gal. 5:22), who through conversion brings back to Christ those living in repentance, and reunites them with Him. And this joy embraces both those in heaven and godly men on earth. That is why there is joy in heaven over one repentant sinner.

While the inexpressible union of the Son of God who gives us repentance and humanity was already being accomplished, and God the Father was mysteriously celebrating His joy over this in heaven, servants were sent out. They were John, the Lord's Forerunner, Zacharias, whom the Jews killed between the altar and the Temple (2 Chr. 24:20–22, Luke 11:51), Simeon, who held God in his arms (Luke 2:28–35), and, in a word, all who announced, before the saving passion and the resurrection, that the Lord's coming to earth in the flesh had already been fulfilled. They were dispatched to summon the guests, that is to say, the Jews (for it is they who were bidden, having been called previously through the prophets). However, they were unwilling to come, in other words, to believe and share in the indescribable communion and grace, even though they had been invited many times beforehand as well as now. "Again", it says – what extraordinary patience! – "he sent forth other servants, saying, Behold, I have prepared my dinner: my oxen and my fatlings are killed, and all things are ready: come unto the marriage" (Matt. 22:4). Some of those that heard made light of it and went off to their farms and their merchandise (Matt. 22:5). Are those who use grape-harvests, vineyards, and problems with their business as an excuse for missing church services, and who are reluctant to listen to the holy psalmody and teaching, any different from them? Others, it says, lay hold on the servants, insulted them and killed them (Matt. 22:6). Not far removed from the latter are those who, in the present day, disobey Church leaders and sometimes speak against them with hostility. But let us freely squeeze the saving juice out of this parable for the sake of such people too.

"Behold", says the king, "I have prepared my finest banquet: my oxen and my fatlings are killed, and all things are ready" (Matt. 22:4). It is a fact that the finest of God's works was accomplished when the Lord became man. Every good and noble thing that God had done for our sake before the Incarnation, as part of His saving plan, was directed towards this end. The most excellent thing of all, or rather, the only truly excellent event beyond compare, was the Incarnation of our Lord Jesus Christ and, even more so, its outcome: the saving passion and the resurrection. The invitation in the Parable apparently took place after the Lord's resurrection, for then it was that all the prerequisites for our salvation were ready: the complete divine plan for the Son of God in the flesh, His divine teaching while incarnate, the consequences of His activity as God and man, the sharing of His divine and human body, the great and holy Sacrifice for our salvation, the resurrection from the dead on the third day, the beginning of eternal life with its godly joy. "My oxen", he says, "and my fatlings are killed." For the old order was united with the new at that time, the new indicated by the sacrifice of calves fattened on grain – for in church now it is bread that is sacrificed for us – and the old by the oxen, transformed into something more divine through the new Sacrifice.

Other servants, the Lord's apostles, were dispatched to preach this message to the Jews as well, while the Master was still forbearing towards them. But when they heard, some did not even attend, as they were wholly taken up with their fields and merchandise, the earth and worldly affairs, whereas others seized the preachers, reviled some and stoned others. As far as their intentions were concerned, they insulted and killed them all. "So the king was angry", it says, "and he sent and destroyed those murderers, and burned up their city" (Matt. 22:7). Since He was still patient even after they had brought about the passion, He sent servants summoning them to repent, proclaiming an amnesty and announcing the bestowal of great and good gifts. They gave guarantees and earnests to this effect, as well as firm assurances. Their hearers, however, not only failed to repent or pay heed, but responded with abuse and repaid the bringers of good tidings with murder. Then the king rightly sent men to destroy them and burn down their city. Everyone knows that these things befell Jerusalem, which the Lord justifiably called a city of murderers (*cf.* Matt. 23:37, Luke 13:34, Isa. 1:21, Jer. 4:31–32).

The people who had been invited, not only now but on many previous occasions, proved themselves unworthy of this calling, and deserving of divine wrath and destruction. So at the Lord's command the same servants, the Lord's apostles, went out into the streets and gathered together, it says, "as many as they found, both bad and good" (Matt. 22:10), and the house was filled with guests. These are those called from among the Gentiles. In those days there was one City of God, Jerusalem, and one Household of God, Israel. Those outside were Gentiles, who were like people flung out into many different streets, for they had numerous and varied beliefs. Those whom the servants found in the highways, and gathered in, are referred to as evil and good on account of the difference in their resolve, as a result of which some were chosen, and their behaviour and way of life were seen to accord with their faith, whereas others were expelled from among the elect, having lived shameful and wicked lives inconsistent with faith.

This is illustrated by what follows. "The king", it says, "came in to see the guests", namely, those of the people invited who had come. His coming in to look at the guests and examine them signifies His appearing at the time of the future Judgment. "And when the king came in to see the guests, he saw there a man which had not on a wedding garment" (Matt. 22:11). Virtue is the spiritual wedding garment, and anyone who has not put it on from now, will not only be found unworthy of that divine bridechamber, but will also experience indescribable bonds and scourging. As every soul has its companion, the body, as its covering, anyone who fails to preserve his body and cleanse it in this life by means of self-control, purity and chastity, will possess it then as a useless garment, unworthy of that incorruptible bridechamber, and the cause of his being thrown out. Once the king, it says, had accused and put to shame the man who was not dressed in a manner worthy of his calling, he told his servants, "Bind him hand and foot, and take him away." In other words, "Surround him with inescapable terrors, and separate him from the dwelling and company of those who rejoice," and "Cast him into outer darkness; there shall be weeping and gnashing of teeth" (Matt. 22:13). He is tightly shackled by the chains of his sins here and now, so it is just that he be bound hand and foot and thrown into outer darkness, going even further away from God, because he did not do works of light in this life. In that place, it tells us, there shall be weeping and gnashing of teeth, for that darkness is not merely darkness, but also unquenchable fire, which is filled, moreover, with unsleeping worms (cf. Mark 9:48, Isa. 66:24).

So there shall be weeping and gnashing of teeth on account of the unbearable sufferings inflicted, which attack both soul and body, the never-ending lamentation and the unceasing regret, which is useless there. After saying these words, the Lord adds, "For many are called, but few are chosen" (Matt. 22:14), to show us that it is not just one particular man who will experience these horrors, but absolutely everyone who is clothed by his deeds in the same depravity. By means of this one individual the Lord sets before us what those evil people are like who, having been called, drawn near and been baptized, have not undergone any change for the better, nor laid aside through repentance the filth that comes from wicked pleasures and passions.

As for us, brethren, let us take off the garment torn to shreds by drunkenness and filling our stomach, and stained by the flesh and its excesses, and let us clothe ourselves, as Isaiah says, "with the garment of salvation and the robe of joy" (Isa. 61:10 Lxx), through self-control and chastity. Let us lay aside the old man, "which is corrupt according to the deceitful lusts" (Eph. 4:22), and put on the new man, which after God is created in holiness and righteousness (*cf.* Eph. 4:24). Let us take off our life's complex covering of rapacity and greed, since it is ugly in God's sight and condemned, and let us put on, as the elect of God, compassion, humility, modesty and meekness (*cf.* Col. 3:12). And let us strive in all ways, according to the apostle's exhortation, to make our calling and election sure (*cf.* 2 Pet. 1:10). By so doing, we shall not fail to attain to the promise of good things to come, and the company of those who rejoice eternally.

May we all attain to this, by the grace and love for mankind of Christ, our spirits' eternal heavenly bridegroom, with whom glory is due to the Father and the Holy Spirit, unto the ages of ages. Amen.

On the Parable of the Sower

OUR LORD JESUS CHRIST chose His disciples not from the wise, not from the noble, not from the rich or the famous, but from among fishermen and tentmakers and poor and illiterate men. This was to make clear to all that neither poverty, nor lack of learning, nor lowly origins, nor anything else of that sort is an impediment to acquiring virtue and understanding the divine sayings and the mysteries of the Spirit. But even the poorest and lowliest and least educated person, if he gives proof of eagerness and an appropriate inclination towards what is good, can not only come to know the divine teaching but also become a teacher himself through God's grace. And the things that hinder us from understanding and grasping the meaning of spiritual teachings are our own indifference and the fact that we cling with all our might to the fleeting concerns of this life. As a result, we do not allow space or time for listening and studying and recalling to mind what we have heard, nor do we care about the things which are to come and things eternal.

Nothing demonstrates this more clearly than today's Gospel reading (Luke 8:5–15). After the Lord had addressed the people using a parable, the disciples approached Him privately and sought to learn the purpose and meaning of the parable He had related on that occasion. They asked why He spoke to the people in parables which were not readily comprehensible. Then the Lord answered them, "Unto you it is given to know the mysteries of the kingdom of God: but to others in parables; that seeing they might not see, and hearing they might not understand" (Luke 8:10).

One might be so bold as to ask Him, "Why is this, Lord? You who are the only Guide of all men, the only universal Master and Provider, only Father and Saviour of all, the light of those lying in the darkness of ignorance, the light that "lighteth every man that cometh into the world" (John 1:9), do You now only illumine Your chosen disciples, and speak obscurely to the rest, lest they should understand and be enlightened?" "Yes", replies the Lord, "man is the only living creature in this world that I wished to create with freedom of choice. I did not come into the world to destroy this handiwork of Mine which had been spoilt, but to rescue it. For that reason, I never draw anyone by force. According to My righteous judgment, only those people who choose, long and seek to put the knowledge of salvation into practice are worthy to be enlightened. 'For every one that asketh receiveth; and he that seeketh findeth; and to him that knocketh it shall be opened' (Luke 11:10). In My surpassing love for mankind, however, I also address those outside this category, without making Myself clear, that I might give them motivation and encouragement to choose and learn how to search out My teaching in order to practice it. For in this way it will be granted to them too to know the mysteries of God's kingdom. This knowledge", He says, "has been given to you who seek more diligently on your own account to put into action what you have learnt. For it is not mere knowledge that is good, but knowledge translated into deeds, and action in accordance with reason. 'For not the hearers of the law', says the Scripture, 'but the doers of the law shall be justified' (Rom. 2:13)."

Do you see, brethren, that the fact that we do not easily understand or grasp the holy teaching is due to our own inaction and indifference? I say this now to your charity, having been appointed as your teacher, for reasons known to the Lord. If anyone is unable to understand the meaning of my teachings in church in all respects, he should come and ask me privately, and with the help of God, who gives me utterance "at the opening of my mouth" (Eph. 6:19), he will hear more clearly and will put what he hears into practice, on account of his persistence in asking.

Let us now look at the parable from the beginning. "A sower went out to sow his seed" (Luke 8:5). The grace of the Spirit rightly ordained that this parable should be read in church in the hearing of all just at this time, for now is the season for sowing, and most people are striving to sow their land with seeds that originate from the earth. Anyone who sows crops every year is sowing perishable seed, which will not sprout unless it dies. Obviously, therefore, he will harvest and reap perishable things, temporary sustenance for the flesh that will soon come to nothing. Through this parable we shall teach you, however, what spiritual and imperishable seeds are, when it is time to sow them, who sows them, and what type of land is able to receive them, so that we may not toil merely in the hope of the harvest which nourishes us for a short time, but may do everything in the hope of that harvest which will provide us with eternal life. "A sower", it says, "went out to sow his seed" (Luke 8:5). Who is he? The Lord Himself, who through the psalmist foretold concerning Himself, "I will open my mouth in parables" (Ps. 78:2 Lxx, Matt. 13:35). But whence did He come out, who is everywhere present? Whither did He come, who is absent from nowhere? Again He said of Himself, "I came forth from the Father, and am come into the world" (John 16:28). Without being separated from the Father's bosom He who is in the world and by whom the world was made (John 1:10), came out and entered the world. He who fills heaven and earth came down from heaven to earth. Consequently, the coming forth of the only-begotten Son of God, and His descent from heaven, represent nothing other than His manifestation in the flesh and His self-emptying, from the unutterable exaltation of divinity down to human nature at the other extreme.

He came out in this way "to sow his seed". What seed is this? The word of instruction, the words of eternal life, the commandments of immortality, the promise of restoration to life, and the gospel of the kingdom of heaven. These all belong to Him, for He said of Himself, "The words that I speak unto you, they are spirit, and they are life" (John 6:63); and Peter told Him, "Thou hast the words of eternal life" (John 6:68). Such seed is His alone and He alone ceaselessly sows it, showing in this way that He is God over all (Rom. 9:5). Every teacher, evangelist and preacher of godliness and pious living also sows the words of life, the word of evangelical and heavenly teaching, but once he has served God's will in his generation he departs, nor did he exist previously. Moreover, the word of salvation which he sows by teaching is not his own but belongs to God, who assists him and "gives utterance at the opening of his mouth" (Eph. 6:19).

Our Lord Jesus Christ, however, being true God, has this seed of eternal life as His own possession, and is always sowing it through the natural law in creation, through the law given in writing to the Israelites, through the prophetic word, and later through the gospel of grace. So the season for such sowing is the entire life-time of every person, or rather, the whole period from the Lord's advent until the end of the world. Harvest time for this seed will be at the Lord's second coming and manifestation, which we await. That is why the apostle says, "He that ploweth should plow in hope" (1 Cor. 9:10), and "He that soweth to the Spirit shall reap life everlasting" (Gal. 6:8). Also the psalmist says, "They that sow in tears" now "shall reap in joy" at that time (Ps. 126:5).

The Lord went out to sow His seed. Where? In people's hearts, for these are the fields which receive spiritual seeds. Some of them resemble a path, as they have been trampled down and pressed solid by evil thoughts and passions, and by the most wicked demons who oversee these things. Those who are like rocky ground are unable, on account of their faint-heartedness and hardness, to hold on to the seeds of teaching to the end, or to bear fruit through them for eternal life. As for those who resemble ground which brings forth thorns, they are intent on possessions and wealth, fleeting pleasures and what springs from these.

Since many differences can be observed between the hearts of men, "A sower", it says, "went out to sow his seed: and as he sowed, some fell by the way side; and it was trodden down, and the fowls of the air devoured it" (Luke 8:5). Some seed, it says, fell beside the path, meaning either into hearts which were outside the right way of the Lord (*cf.* Acts 13:10), in which case it was trampled underfoot by the evil demons who walk about in trackless places, or else into hearts on the demons' evil path, such that the birds, the evil spirits in the air, ate it up and destroyed it; and so it is as though these people never heard God's word at all. "Those by the way side are they that hear; then cometh the devil, and taketh away the word out of their hearts, lest they should believe and be saved" (Luke 8:12). "And some fell", it says, "upon a rock" (Luke 8:6), though Matthew says, "upon stony places" (Matt. 13:5), meaning, on a hard unyielding heart within which the word cannot develop, or take a vigorous hold, or put down roots. So "as soon as it was sprung up", it says, "it withered away, because it lacked moisture" (Luke 8:6). That is to say, they endured for a while, and seemed to grow to some extent, then when temptations came upon them they disappeared, as they were incapable of bringing fruit to perfection, because of the weakness of their resolve. "They on the rock are they, which, when they hear, receive the word with joy; and these have no root, which for a while believe, and in time of temptation fall away" (Luke 8:13). "And some fell among thorns" (Luke 8:7), hearts entirely devoted to the fleeting material things of this life, and submerged in the concerns and delights which come from them. Once such thorns have grown up alongside the seed, they choke and obliterate it completely. "That which fell among thorns are they, which, when they have heard, go forth, and are choked with cares and riches and pleasures of this life, and bring no fruit to perfection" (Luke 8:14).

In this way, the Lord casts out and rejects those who pay no attention to the divine Spirit's teaching (the ones who fall by the wayside), and those who take notice but only for a short time (those who resemble stony ground), and also those who accept and retain a knowledge of it, but are corrupted by wealth and glory and self-indulgence (these are the fields full of thorns). He then uses the parable to introduce and set before us those people well-pleasing to God, saying, "Other fell on good ground" (Luke 8:8), that is to say, a soul with a good and noble disposition, which eagerly receives the word of instruction and holds on to it, without allowing itself to be used as a channel for the enemies of its salvation to pass through, and which patiently watches over it, resolutely holding fast to what it has heard, bearing temptations with fortitude. Rejecting a fleeting life devoted to money-making and enjoyment, it matures and bears fruit, which, in the words of the divine Mark, "sprang up and increased; and brought forth, some thirty, and some sixty, and some an hundred" (Mark 4:8).

It would be possible to call these categories servitude, work for wages, and sonship. When at first someone approaches God as a guilty man, he really is a slave on account of his former disobedience and defiance. Next, having served as a slave, he desires a recompense as well. Then, after making progress in love, he becomes a son, who is now in possession of virtue and submits as if by nature to the heavenly Father, without compulsion. Let us strive, brethren, either to lay claim to divine sonship by loving God and refraining from everything else, through continuous prayer and psalmody, and waiting upon Him without distraction, or else to be classed with the hired workers, who successfully achieve self-control in all aspects of the struggle, or else to be numbered among the slaves mourning their former sins. Anyone who does not fall into one of these three groups is not among those being saved.

"When he had said these things", it says, "the Lord cried, He that hath ears to hear, let him hear" (Luke 8:8). This is not because some people do not have ears, but because not everyone has ears for the purpose of hearing the word of salvation. Since, as the saying goes, "It is the mind which sees and the mind which hears", those who have ears to hear are the ones who listen with their minds and with understanding. If it is also the case that "a good understanding have all they that do his commandments" (Ps. 111:10), and the word is recognized through deeds, it is not simply the listener who has ears to hear, but the obedient man who puts what he hears into practice.

Before all else, brethren, I beseech you, let us hear with understanding that the Lord did not say that He went out to plough the human fields, or to break up the ground two or three times, dig up the roots of the weeds and smooth out the clods of earth, that is to say, to prepare our hearts for cultivation, but that He went out immediately to sow. Why? Because this preliminary work on our souls prior to sowing ought to be done by us. That is why the Forerunner of the gospel of grace, anticipating this fact, says with a loud voice, "Prepare ye the way of the Lord, make his paths straight" (Matt. 3:3), and "Repent ye: for the kingdom of heaven is at hand" (Matt. 3:2). Our preparation and the starting point of repentance is blaming ourselves, confession, and abstention from evil. He also issued a warning to those who had not made themselves ready in this way to bear fruits worthy of repentance (*cf.* Matt. 3:8, Luke 3:8). "Every tree which bringeth not forth good fruit is hewn down, and cast into the fire" (Matt. 3:10). The sentence God passes on unrepentant sinners is that they be cut off, that once they have been torn away from this present life and the life to come, they be despatched, alas, to unquenchable hell-fire.

Let us repent, brethren, and display fruits worthy of repentance. Let each of us abstain from his wicked ways, and let us learn to speak and do what is good. Let us prepare ourselves to receive the heavenly seed, the word of life. Let us restrain our tongue from evils (What sort of evils? Idle words, abuse, slander), and our lips from uttering oaths, lies and foolish speech. Perhaps these are the evil birds mentioned in the parable, who eat up the good seed and bring it to nought. For every word is like a flying bird, which is why some have referred to them as "having wings". An evil word let loose through the mouth from its nest in the evil treasure of a man's heart (*cf.* Matt. 12:35) robs the soul of its sanctification. The Lord says elsewhere on this subject, "Those things which proceed out of the mouth defile the man" (Matt. 15:18). May no corrupt words come out of your mouth, but only such as are capable of giving edification to those listening.

None of you should be so engrossed in the concerns of this life that you are somehow turned into stone by them and cannot open your ears and heart to the dew of the words of the Spirit's teaching. Why is it that when the earth receives rain it is loosened, softened and enriched, but fired clay stays hard and dry and does not dissolve?

Is it not because the earth is warmed but not burnt by the sun's rays, and so has its pores open to receive moisture, whereas the earthenware has been burnt through forcible contact with fire, and has its pores tightly closed and sealed deep down, so that it cannot let in even the finest rain? In the same way, when anyone is obsessed by the bodily, earthly cares of everyday life his heart is continuously and severely hardened. Deadened in his understanding even before he returns to the ground, he is incapable of any perception of divine teaching. On the other hand, he who deals with the world as though he had no dealings with it, according to the apostle's advice (1 Cor. 7:31), will be ready to seek heavenly things, listen to them with understanding, and zealously and eagerly act upon them. He will not merely hear, but retain inwardly and put into practice, that he may be called blessed by the Lord for being like the faithful and wise servant (*cf.* Matt. 24:45–46). "Whosoever heareth these sayings of mine", says the Lord, "and doeth them, I will liken him unto a wise man" (Matt. 7:24).

If any of you amuses himself with gluttony, excessive drinking, self-indulgent pleasure and drunkenness, he should stop. Otherwise he receives the heavenly seed, the words of instruction, to no avail, and will not be shown to be a fruitful field for God. You all know that when sown fields are too wet they cannot produce crops. So how can a heart sodden with self-indulgence and wine-drinking display heavenly fruit? If anyone has fallen into any sort of impure fornication, let him turn back, give it up, and cleanse himself through repentance. "Shall he fall, and not arise? shall he turn away, and not return?" (Jer. 8:4). If he wallows in this filth, how can he keep safe within him the holy myrrh which he receives, the pearl of great price (Matt. 13:46), by which I mean the word of salvation. Pearls are not given to pigs (*cf.* Matt. 7:6), and people in their right mind do not mix myrrh with mud. If someone poured out myrrh and mingled it with dung, and put it into a dirty container, he would make the myrrh useless and ruin it. Even though holy myrrh cannot be damaged, anyone who approaches it without abstaining from impurity can be sure of suffering the harm it would have suffered, had it been capable of being spoilt. Whoever is greedy for gain, let him be so no longer, but share what he has with those who have nothing. Unless he does so, he will not escape God's anger, and if he cannot get away from the divine wrath, how can he receive the holy seed? To those who asked John, the Lord's Forerunner, how to flee from the wrath to come, he replied, "He that hath two coats, let him impart to him that hath none; and he that hath meat, let him do likewise" (Luke 3:11).

In a word, let each one of you, through repentance, pull up by the roots the thorns and thistles of sin that you have nurtured in yourself through a life full of passions and pleasures. By so doing, you will cultivate your field and make yourself ready to receive the saving seed. Then once you have received it, you will bring to perfection the fruit of eternal life. Not only ought we to give up our physical desires for the sake of that life, but even, if need be, our soul, for thus we shall follow in the Master's footsteps, be partakers of the glory and kingdom which are in Christ, and live with Him for ever, glorified with Him.

Our irrefutable witness is the most excellent of martyrs, the wonderworker and myrrh-gusher Demetrius, before whose icon kings and priests prostrate themselves and rejoice to be present, for he followed in the Lord's footsteps by the way he lived, by his words and his sufferings. Not just anyone will be acceptable to him as a participant in the festival and the ceremony which has already been announced, but only those who have already been initiated into repentance. Given that the saint left behind every material attachment and showed himself in his entirety to be, in Paul's words, "a sweet savour of Christ" (2 Cor. 2:15), to the point that, after his struggle, even his coffin became a fount of fragrant myrrh, how can he allow anyone to dance around him and sing to him who smells of the stuff of passions and reeks of the unhealed wounds of sin? "Praise is out of place on the lips of sinners", says the Scripture (Ecclus. 15:9). As we celebrate the forefeast, let us also purify ourselves in advance of the appointed feast of the Greatmartyr, which is drawing near. Then, having rejoiced in spirit together with him at the memory of his struggles for Christ's sake, his Christlike life beforehand, and his rewards from Christ afterwards, may we receive this pledge of our hope to dwell in heaven with those who rejoice eternally.

May we all attain to this by the prayers of our city's patron saint and martyr for Christ, to the glory of the Father and the Son and the Holy Spirit, now and for ever and unto the ages of ages. Amen.

On the Parable of Lazarus and the Rich Man

WE EACH HAVE some of our physical necessities as a result of our own labours, but the rest we receive by exchanging what we have with one another. Clerks, farmers, tailors, weavers, builders, shoemakers, doctors and so on, are not the same. So, as no one on his own has all the necessary things, although everyone inevitably needs them all, currency was invented as a means by which, to improve life, surplus could be disposed of and needs met. The farmer offers his excess produce to people who do not cultivate the land, and when he has received the proceeds he uses them to buy a house, perhaps, or clothes. The shoemaker sells shoes, and on receipt of the appropriate price he provides himself with whatever he needs and lacks. Thus our lives consist of mutual sharing between us all, which is why we have settlements and towns, and man is a social animal.

With regard to spiritual matters and the pursuit of virtue, however, this does not apply. Someone who is chaste but not righteous cannot give a righteous man some of his own chastity and acquire righteousness from him. Nor can someone who tells the truth but bears grudges ever make an exchange with someone else to obtain forbearance; nor can he pass on the truthfulness of his speech to another person who lacks veracity. There is no coin or any other such means in these cases to quantify the exchanges between the two parties and make them of equal value. For that reason, brethren, it is an absolute necessity for each of us to practise every virtue. If anyone fails in one of them he cannot receive it from anyone else, nor escape condemnation and punishment for his shortcoming. As David says, "A brother cannot redeem, shall a stranger redeem him?" (*cf.* Ps. 49:7 Lxx), implying, "nobody".

But see how great is Christ the Lord's indescribable love for mankind! That which cannot be received even in exchange for the soul's virtues, which are worth the same and truly precious, He has made easy to buy in another way. Our lowly, earthly, bodily needs, namely, food and drink, clothing, the gold and silver each one possesses: all such things are earth and dust, and nothing is less valuable than that. Yet these worthless things can be the means by which, if, in accordance with the Lord's promise and exhortation, someone offers what he has in excess to those possessed of virtues (because they are completely destitute of physical necessities), he can make up for his deficiency in virtues and escape punishment for being without them through this act of giving. To demonstrate this point, the great Paul, writing to the Corinthians, calls such sharing "fellowship with the saints" (*cf.* 2 Cor. 8:4), and goes on to say, "that your abundance may be a supply for their want, that their abundance also may be a supply for your want" (2 Cor. 8:14). And the Lord says, "Make to yourselves friends of the mammon of unrighteousness; that, when ye fail, they may receive you into everlasting habitations" (Luke 16:9), using the expression, "mammon of unrighteousness" to mean what is over and above our requirements and is not passed on to those in need.

Each of us, brethren, must, as I have said, practise every virtue, but if we lack one of them, we have to make up for what is missing by sharing what we have. This is the next best way of fulfilling Christ's word – especially for you who pass your lives in the world – and by it we can secure the salvation of your souls. If, however, we neglect this way as well, it is greatly to be feared that unquenchable fire and everlasting deprivation may take possession of us. To make this clear, the Lord set before us the parable which was read today in church. "There was a certain rich man, which was clothed in purple and fine linen, and fared sumptuously every day" (Luke 16:19). All the rich man's attention was on clothing, adornment, extravagant garments, eating, drinking and pleasures. "And there was a certain beggar named Lazarus, which was laid at his gate, full of sores, and desiring to be fed with the crumbs which fell from the rich man's table: moreover the dogs came and licked his sores" (Luke 16:20–21).

Do you observe how the rich man had absolutely nothing in common with Lazarus? He gorged himself daily and his table was full of all sorts of luxurious foods and sauces, whereas Lazarus, who had never eaten his fill, longed to satisfy his hunger even with the plainest fare. He was resplendent, dressed in purple and fine linen, and his excellent physical health served to make him more handsome. By contrast, even the tattered rags Lazarus had round him were soiled and ill-smelling as he had broken out in sores and was bleeding all over. The rich man was seated high up, surrounded by a crowd of attendants, but Lazarus was lying on the ground where he had fallen, by the gate, and had no one even to chase the dogs away.

Why does the Lord call the poor man by name, but make the rich man anonymous? It could be said that this poor man's name is written in the heavens, as the Scripture says (*cf.* Luke 10:20), whereas the rich man's name and memory have been blotted out from there and destroyed. The psalmist says of such people, "I will not take up their names into my lips" (Ps. 16:4). Also, since every wealthy person can understand the parable as referring to himself, and can find a motive for repentance by regarding himself as the rich man, he was introduced without a name, so that the account could apply to everyone well-to-do. Not every poor man, however, can think of himself as Lazarus, even if he resembles him, for he must wait humbly for the Lord's verdict. For that reason, the poor man is referred to by name.

"And it came to pass, that the beggar died, and was carried by the angels into Abraham's bosom" (Luke 16:22). With honour beyond what the earth can offer, the poor man is led away like an athlete towards crowns of victory. Having showed us the rich man who is not saved, the Lord immediately presents us with a rich man who is, for such is Abraham. He does not refer to him as rich, however, because his virtue was greater than his wealth. He showed a father's loving disposition to everybody, and was therefore named after his most precious possession, his virtue, for "Abraham" means "father of many" (*cf.* Gen. 17:5). That other rich man, by contrast, had nothing superior to earthly, fleeting riches, and so was named after them. It was not, however, on account of his wealth that he failed to be saved, but because of his love of pleasure, hard-heartedness and lack of hospitality. Abraham, too, was prosperous, but by means of his love for God, his compassion, and his hospitality to strangers, he was not only saved but became a place for others being saved. So when Lazarus died he was carried by the angels – for, according to Paul, they are ministers "for them who shall be heirs of salvation" (Heb. 1:14) – and was brought by them to Abraham's bosom, which is the land of the living, the dwelling of those who rejoice for ever, and the realm of everlasting blessings.

"The rich man", it says, "also died, and was buried" (Luke 16:22). Perhaps when Lazarus died he did not even have a grave, as there was no one to bury him. No mention at all is made of a grave in his case, but the account then goes on to say that the rich man "was buried". Another reason this is mentioned is because of the ostentation and extravagance which extends even to the tombs of the wealthy, but the graves of such men become, alas, their doorway to hell and the torments of the nethermost parts of the earth. For, it says, the rich man was buried, "And in hell he lift up his eyes, being in torments, and seeth Abraham afar off, and Lazarus in his bosom" (Luke 16:23). There was a time when the rich man had seen Lazarus cast down in front of the gate, a victim of hunger, writhing on the ground in the dust unable even to move, and he turned a blind eye. Now that he is lying in the depths being tortured and cannot escape his torments, he looks up and sees Lazarus comfortably settled high above, passing his time in profound ease and dwelling in Abraham's bosom, and instead of resolving to ignore him, he thinks he has a right not be overlooked by the man he formerly disregarded. In the place where mercy belonged, he had neither looked for it nor practised it, but there where justice is merciless he seeks mercy to no avail. "He cried and said, Father Abraham, have mercy on me, and send Lazarus, that he may dip the tip of his finger in water, and cool my tongue; for I am tormented in this flame" (Luke 16:24). He restricted his plea to something extremely trivial, not daring to ask for more as his conscience condemned him.

He shouted because of the great distance between them, and he is shown calling Abraham his father so we might learn that he belonged to the race of God-fearing men and not suppose that he was being roasted alive for impiety. For it was because he was unmerciful and pleasure-loving that he was surrounded by the unquenchable flames of fire, although he was related to Abraham by blood. "Have mercy on me", he said, "for I am in torment, and send Lazarus" (Luke 16:24), to whom he had shown no pity when he was suffering in front of his gate. That is why he does not direct the supplication to Lazarus. He asks for a drop of water, a minute quantity to cool his tongue, and he does not obtain it. Do you see how his punishment pays him back with interest? In the days when Lazarus was poor, he could not eat his fill of the crumbs which fell from the rich man's table, but now the rich man is not only deprived of a full stomach and luxuries, but is not even deemed worthy of a tiny drop of water. For, says the parable, "Abraham said, Son, remember that thou in thy lifetime receivedst thy good things, and likewise Lazarus evil things: but now he is comforted, and thou art tormented" (Luke 16:25).

Abraham feels sorry for the rich man in the flames, and sympathetically calls him "Son". In my opinion, however, he pities him not so much for his punishment as for the evil still at work in him. For he has not yet reached an awareness of his sins, nor does he understand yet that it is just that he should burn. The rich man does not say, "Have mercy on me, for I have kindled this fire and stored up these torments for myself. Instead of the sound of flutes, hand-clapping and disgusting songs, I now hear shouts, wailing and the horrible noise of the fire raging around me. Instead of sweet fragrances I smell the fumes from the fire, instead of abundant food and drink and the pleasures they brought, I now have my tongue utterly parched by this fire and am without even a drop of water. Instead of the flames of impure passion, the fire consumes my whole body." He does not say these things, but merely bewails his torments. How does Abraham reply to him? "Come to your senses. Confess that you were rightly consigned to the fire, remembering that during your lifetime you received all those things which you considered good for you to have, and which you chose to acquire rather than other things which were put within your grasp. The benefits you strove for, which were transitory ones, you obtained, as you preferred them to eternal blessings. On the other hand", says Abraham, "Lazarus experienced those evils which were the opposite of your own good fortune, that is to say, bodily afflictions. So now he is eternally consoled for having temporarily suffered then, whereas you are unceasingly afflicted because in those days you enjoyed yourself for a while and revelled in luxury."

Why does Abraham use the word meaning "you received your due" rather than simply "you received"? To show us that anyone who devotes himself in this life to pleasures and self-indulgence, who has plenty of money to spend and makes bad use of his wealth, will receive no reward even if he manages to do some good. Instead of a reward he has his present abundance and ease. In the same way, someone who is worn down by poverty and illness, and bears it courageously, has his bodily suffering as payment for his faults.

"Beside all this", says Abraham, "between us and you there is a great gulf fixed: so that they which would pass from hence to you cannot; neither can they pass to us, that would come from thence" (Luke 16:26). Do you see that even Abraham himself cannot help those condemned to that place even if he wanted to? For, he says, the intervening chasm is impassable, so that those who wish to cross over are unable. "Neither can they pass to us", he says, "that would come from thence." It seems there are other condemned people who are even deeper within the flames, whom Abraham speaks of as those "from thence", who are even more severely tormented by the fire of hell and cannot speak at all. Perhaps they are wealthy men who grew rich not only by failing to share with others but also by extortionate means, which is not something the rich man in the parable is accused of. He is not condemned for being greedy for gain or unjust, but solely for being unmerciful and pleasure-loving. Abraham tells him, "As you preferred a fleeting, comfortable life devoted to enjoyment rather than self-control, it is just that pain, suffering and affliction should now encompass you. You never shared with the poor by giving, nor did you acquire friends through unrighteous mammon, nor did you offer what you had over and above your needs to those in want, but you remained without any fellowship at all with the saints, setting yourself as far apart from them as evil is from virtue. That is why a great gulf has been fixed between us who lived virtuously and you who spent your lives in wickedness, such that no one can ever cross over from one side to the other." These words of his are proof that the damnation of sinners is unending and unchanging, as is the comfort of the righteous.

In his foolishness the rich man neither understands, nor stops sinning, nor condemns himself. Still attempting to justify himself, as though nobody had testified to him beforehand about this place of torment, he says, "I pray thee therefore, father, that thou wouldest send him to my father's house: for I have five brethren; that he may testify unto them, lest they also come into this place of torment" (Luke 16:27–28). He explains that if he had had someone to give him the evidence beforehand, he would not have done those things for which he was sentenced to hell. Abraham replied, "They have Moses and the prophets; let them hear them" (Luke 16:29) – for Moses says in his song, as if on God's behalf, "A fire is kindled in mine anger, and shall burn unto the lowest hell" (Deut. 32:22), and Isaiah, in harmony with the other prophets, says, "The lawless and sinners shall burn together, and none shall quench them" (Isa. 1:31 Lxx). When Abraham had said these words, the rich man objected once more, saying, "Nay, father Abraham: but if one went unto them from the dead, they will repent" (Luke 16:30). What is Abraham's answer to this? "If they hear not Moses and the prophets", he says, "neither will they be persuaded, though one rose from the dead" (Luke 16:31), as though he were actually telling him, "Before you died you took no notice of the words of Moses or the prophets, so even if you had seen someone who had risen from the dead you would not have been convinced by him to give up your dissolute and cruel way of life. That is why you are now rightly engulfed by the fire of hell and suffer unremitting agonies without mercy."

That rich man, brethren, who had Moses and the prophets, none of whom had risen from the dead, seems to have had some sort of excuse. We, by contrast, hear, along with them, Him who rose from the dead for our sake, saying, "Lay not up for yourselves treasures upon earth, but lay up for yourselves treasures in heaven" (Matt. 6:19, 20), "Give to him that asketh thee, and from him that would borrow of thee turn not thou away" (Matt. 5:42), and "Give alms of such things as ye have; and, behold, all things are clean unto you" (Luke 11:41). If someone eats and drinks with drunkards but is hard hearted to the poor and gives them nothing, "The Lord", says the Scripture, "will come in a day when he looketh not for him, and at an hour when he is not aware, and will cut him in sunder, and will appoint him his portion with the unbelievers" (Luke 12:46).

There is no longer any excuse for you and, since "a man's life consisteth not in the abundance of the things which he possesseth" (Luke 12:15), anyone who has anything extra should share it with those who are without, and by so doing he will be adopted into the inheritance of Abraham, the father of those on the way to salvation. As for the needy, they should emulate the patient endurance of Lazarus, gaining their souls with their patience (*cf.* Luke 21:19), and winning a place for themselves in Abraham's bosom, whence "all pain, sorrow and sighing have fled" (Isa. 35:10; 51:11 Lxx, *cf.* Rev. 21:4), and where godly delight, enjoyment and bliss dwell without end. For this reason, Christ revealed to us, through this parable, what it was like there, so that after we have improved through repentance He might vouchsafe us those eternal pleasures, and deliver us from the torments in store for sinners. But if we do not grow better by means of repenting, there is a fearful risk that we may increase the torments inflicted on us. "That servant", it says, "which knew his lord's will, but did not do it, shall be beaten with many stripes" (*cf.* Luke 12:47).

Having addressed us in these and similar words and given us His evidence, He who suffered, was buried and rose from the dead for our sake then ascended into heaven. He appointed a countless host of witnesses to His coming and to the truth of His pronouncements. Among those, if anyone stands out conspicuously as more excellent than most, it is the supremely great Demetrius, whom our Church sets before us now as the cause for our celebration, and who not only declared his testimony in words, but resisted the unbelievers to the point of shedding his blood. He showed his body to be an indestructible pillar which in its own right traces out for us the Saviour's sufferings and presents them before our eyes, and by the myrrh and miracles that stream from this body of his he preaches both the resurrection of Him who was crucified and the power of the risen Lord. For how could the saint who imitated His passion and died for Him be counted worthy of such glory unless He who rose "reigneth as Lord", according to the Psalter, and "is clothed with majesty and hath girded himself with almighty power" (*cf.* Ps. 93:1), as the only-begotten Son of the Father.

With our eyes on the martyr who bore witness to the truth, let us obey the Truth Himself by living in a way pleasing to God. Keeping the feast with our souls as well as our bodies, let us approach Demetrius, the finest of noble saints, that strengthened by him in soul, body, mind and senses, we may think on the blessedness stored up in heaven for those who live godly lives here, and long for it and seek after it to the end through our actions.

May we all attain to this by the grace and love for mankind of our Lord and God and Saviour, Jesus Christ, to whom belong glory, power, honour and worship, together with His Father without beginning and the life-giving Spirit, now and for ever and unto the ages of ages. Amen.